F/A-18
HORNET

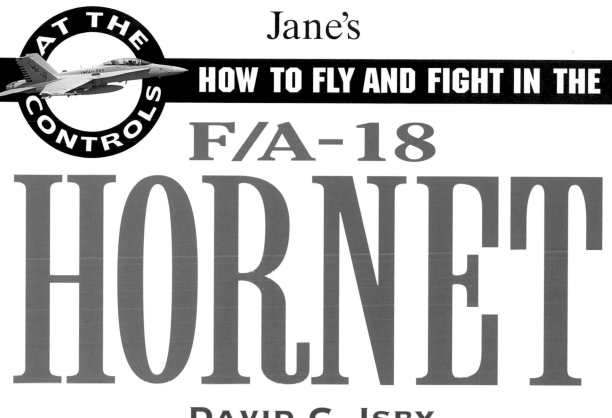

AT THE CONTROLS

Jane's

HOW TO FLY AND FIGHT IN THE

F/A-18
HORNET

DAVID C. ISBY

HarperCollins*Publishers*

In the USA for information address:
HarperCollins*Publishers* Inc.
10 East 53rd Street
New York
NY 10022

In the UK for information address:
HarperCollins*Publishers*
77-85 Fulham Palace Road
Hammersmith
London W6 8JB

First Published in Great Britain by
HarperCollins*Publishers* 1997

1 3 5 7 9 10 8 6 4 2

Copyright © David C. Isby

ISBN 0 00 472009 1

Editor: Ian Drury
Design: Rod Teasdale
Color artwork: John Ridyard
Production: Ken Clark

Colour reproduction by Colourscan
Printed in Italy by Rotolito

CONTENTS

INTRODUCTION:
HORNET MISSION

Flying a fighter in combat, especially air-to-air combat, is a remote experience even for those who have trained for it much of their lives. Only two F/A-18 pilots have ever fired in anger at enemy aircraft: the result was two Iraqi MiG-21s splashed. Others have attacked ground targets, either in Iraq and Kuwait or in Bosnia. But most F/A-18 pilots, like the vast majority of those who have achieved the sought-after status of fighter pilot over the past 50 years, have never been in combat. Those who keep the fighters flying or pay the bills for them are even more remote from the "sharp end".

This book is an attempt to bring the experience of taking an F/A-18 on a combat mission to those who would otherwise not have the chance. It is a view from the cockpit, showing what the pilot of one F/A-18, on one sortie in a future conflict, sees and does. *At The Controls* is intended to give the reader a "hands-on" experience of what it is like to fight and fly in one specific US Navy McDonnell Douglas F/A-18C Hornet fighter/attack aircraft on a hypothetical combat mission in the immediate future. The

Above: Marine Corps humor: Major J A Stout's call-sign is 'Guinness', honoring Ireland's famous brew.

Below: The next generation is to be represented by the F/A-18E Super Hornet, seen here making its first flight from St Louis on 29 November 1995.

Above: The 'green jacket' prepares this F/A-18C of VFA-86 for launch from USS America (CV-66). The nosewheel tow-bar has been attached to the catapult shuttle, while the hold-back restrains the aircraft.

Left: The Hornet set the pattern for later fighter cockpits, with three multi-function colour displays, and hands-on-throttle-and-stick (HOTAS) controls.

Above: Potential threats to US Navy carriers include the Tupolev Tu-22M Backfire, equipped with supersonic anti-ship missiles, and with a dash speed of 1,080 knots (2,000 km/hr).

Below: The two-seat F/A-18D is used by the USMC both for crew training and for the night attack role, in which it replaces the A-6E. VMFA(AW)-224 is based at MCAS Beaufort, South Carolina.

view is not limited to what the pilot can see. In addition to what the pilot sees in the cockpit during the mission, there is the larger situation to be considered. The operational context of the F/A-18's mission and the capabilities of its enemies are key parts of the process.

The point of view of the reader will be that of the F/A-18's pilot. The reader will "fly along", watching and listening. Those who would win — or even survive — in post-modern warfare must successfully exploit evolving technology in tactical situations more stressing, dynamic, and multifaceted than anything imagined back in the Cold War. *At The Controls* gives the reader a detailed example of how one F/A-18 pilot would

Above: This F/A-18D of VMFA(AW)-224 looks somewhat ungainly with its undercarriage down. The mainwheels are located well aft of the centre of gravity to ensure stability on a highly mobile deck.

An F/A-18A of VMFA-134 'Smokers': a Marine Air Reserve Unit, based at NAS Miramar, CA. Its two-tone camouflage suggests association with the Navy's 'Top Gun' air combat school.

apply this technology. For the sake of simplicity, the pilot in this mission is a 'he', but, as revealed below, flying the F/A-18 is no longer a male preserve.

The tale starts with the airplane and the pilot as separate stories. The F/A-18 came to be on this carrier flight deck through a long process, starting with its development in the 1970s. The pilot got to be there by going through a grueling training pipeline. Put together, airplane and pilot become a fighting unit. Combined with a wingman, they become 'Nickel Flight', which is part of a strike with over two dozen different aircraft. This, in turn, is an instrument of US national policy at the highest level.

Above: This photograph of the first F/A-18E fuselage illustrates the large area devoted to access panels. Accurate alignment of the various modules during assembly is ensured by a computer-based laser system.

Left: This white early production F/A-18B is assigned to the US Naval Test Pilot School at Patuxent River, Maryland, where new aircraft are tested by the Naval Air Warfare Center.

CAPABILITIES:
HORNET F/A-18 ROLE EVALUATION

The F/A-18 is the mainstay of the US Navy's carrier air wings and the US Marine Corps' fighter squadrons. The F/A-18 is a 1970s design, but being the last of its contemporaries — the F-14, F-15, F-16, and Tornado — to enter service it has the advantage of using more advanced technologies, especially in areas such as cockpit design.

Below: Three F/A-18Ds of VMFA(AW)-224 are joined on patrol by an F/A-18A of VMFA-122 'Crusaders', which is likewise based at MCAS Beaufort.

The F/A-18 was developed from the Northrop YF-17, an experimental USAF fighter that lost out to the F-16 in competition for that service's order. The Navy, impressed by its twin-engine design, ordered it to replace its F-4 fighters and A-7 attack aircraft and supplement its high-cost F-14 fighters.

The first F/A-18 flew in 1978, and the single-seat F/A-18A and two-seat F/A-18B entered service in 1980. The F/A-18 has been improved throughout its life. F/A-18C/D models replaced the F/A-18A/Bs in front-line US service after the Cold War. New, advanced models — the single-seat F/A-18E and the two-seat F/A-18F — will enter service in the late 1990s.

The F/A-18 differs from the 1950s and 1960s designs it replaced. Its improved performance allows it to take advantage of technological improvements in engine, sensor, and weapons technology. One aircraft — the F/A-18 — can today carry out missions which before had required multiple specialized aircraft. The unique split "F/A" designation shows that it is intended to be equally capable for both air-to-air and air-to-surface missions.

Any aircraft design is a compromise. The F/A-18 cannot defeat incoming aircraft and missiles at long range as successfully as the F-14. Nor can it haul vast amounts of bombs at long range in all weathers as capably as the

A-6 attack aircraft. But for the US Navy, where the number of different aircraft that can be fit onto each carrier is, of necessity, finite, versatility is greatly valued. In the skies over Iraq and Bosnia, the F/A-18 has proven highly capable, primarily air to ground but also in the air-to-air mission. Over Iraq, the two F/A-18s that shot down MiG-21s did so without having to jettison their external bombloads.

Today, the F/A-18 represents the state of the art in modern combat aircraft. But the shape of its successors is already evident. Future fighters such as the F-22 will emphasize reduced radar and infrared signatures ("stealth"), will make use of structural composite materials, and will cruise at supersonic speeds without afterburner. The F/A-18 represents a bridge between combat aircraft as they were in the years of the Cold War and how they will be in the future.

Above: An F/A-18D of VMFA(AW)-553 'Hawks' fires a laser-guided Hughes AGM-65E Maverick missile.

Left: Flying low over the desert, this F/A-18D of VMFA(AW)-224 is carrying a typical load of 'iron' bombs. The soot around the upper nose indicates that the 20mm Gatling gun has recently been fired.

THE HORNET: READY FOR BATTLE

Each aspect of the F/A-18's design reflects its missions and design compromises made to permit maximum performance within weight, volume and (as ever) cost constraints.

The F/A-18's two engines — essential for an airplane that does most of its flying over water — are afterburning General Electric F404 turbofans. Their advanced technology allows both rapid acceleration — unlike early turbofans — and economical cruise performance. Despite this, twin-engine F/A-18s are thirsty beasts, especially when carrying a heavy bombload. The need to pack a lot of capability in a small volume for carrier operations means it does not have the internal fuel capacity of larger twin-engine fighters such as the USAF's F-15. As a result, offensive F/A-18 operations usually involve air refueling. This may lead the battle group to come as close inshore as the threat permits to reduce the strain on tanker resources.

One area where the F/A-18 differs from its contemporaries is top speed. The F/A-18's maximum high-altitude dash speed, Mach 1.8, is less than that of the F-15 or F-16, both of which exceed Mach 2. This capability was found to be so rarely used that the Navy did not want to invest in the "cost" of engine design (including permitting the use of fixed ramp air intake) to make it possible. Such high-speed dashes are rare, and only carried out without external stores. One of the few times when it does come in handy is when disengaging from air combat, but even the fastest fighter cannot outrun an air-to-air missile.

While many F/A-18s — especially those in the Australian, Canadian, and Spanish air arms — seldom go near the water, the aircraft's design has been shaped by its requirement to fly from US carriers. The F/A-18 is a naval aircraft, as evidenced by massive flaps, reinforced landing gear, and tailhook along with a strengthened structure (with the weight penalty these entail). Its small wings have modest sweepback, but all of the leading edge is variable, allowing it to, in effect, shift forward to provide additional lift. The need to have these capabilities as an integral part of the design is one reason why few aircraft have been successful in carrier operations unless designed for it from the start.

The F/A-18 pilot, the joke goes, is not in charge, but only a voting member of a committee that includes the position sensors,

Moveable leading edge in take-off position

Aileron

Slotted flap

Fin

Rudder

Air brake

Taileron

General Electric F404 engines with afterburners and variable area tailpipes

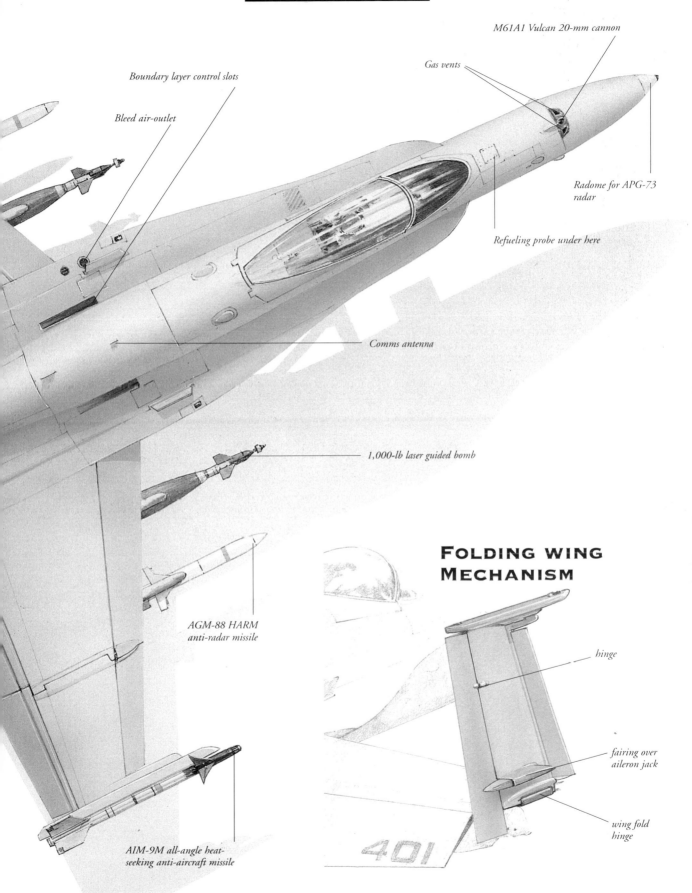

M61A1 Vulcan 20-mm cannon

Gas vents

Boundary layer control slots

Bleed air-outlet

Radome for APG-73 radar

Refueling probe under here

Comms antenna

1,000-lb laser guided bomb

FOLDING WING MECHANISM

AGM-88 HARM anti-radar missile

hinge

fairing over aileron jack

wing fold hinge

AIM-9M all-angle heat-seeking anti-aircraft missile

401

Ready for action on the aicraft carrier Nimitz in the Gulf War.

M61 20MM CANNON

rotating barrels

pivot for refueling probe deployment mechanism

gear box   *electric motor*

magazine (540 rounds)

breech mechanism

duct for spent cartridges

F/A-18 HORNET

This Hornet is ready for take off, armed and waiting for the tower to give them clearance. The deck crew will be doing final checks on the catapult and then the yellow jackets will give them the signal.

force sensors, and flight control computers. The F/A-18 makes more use of external sensors and automatic modes of operation than aircraft designed even a few years ago, such as the F-15. While the pilot retains full manual override authority, these systems have the potential to help reduce pilot workload.

The vast array of electronics the F/A-18 carries, concealed beneath radomes and low-drag antennas, is a reminder that the US Navy remains one of the most technologically-advanced fighting forces in the world today. It has long known that to control the sea it must first control the air, and to control both it must first control the electromagnetic spectrum.

The F/A-18's electronics include both the APG-73 multimode radar that detects air and surface targets and the AAS-38B Nite Hawk forward looking infra red (FLIR) sensor that identifies surface targets by day or night. For night operations, an AAR-50 Thermal Imaging Navigation System (TINS) pod is available. This provides an infrared overlay of the visual scene outside the cockpit, projected on the Head-Up Display (HUD). The pilot can also wear night vision goggles (NVGs). These capabilities allow the F/A-18 to take full advantage of weapons more effective than those envisioned when it was designed in the 1970s.

Hard to see, but equally vital, is the F/A-18's defensive electronic warfare equipment. This includes the transmitter for the ALQ-126 jammer, the upper and lower IFF response antennas (which respond to IFF challenges with a coded electronic signal), the multiple antennas for the ALR-67 radar homing and warning (RHAW) system, and the ALE-47 chaff and flare dispenser.

The F/A-18 must be able to communicate as well as fight. In addition to VHF and UHF

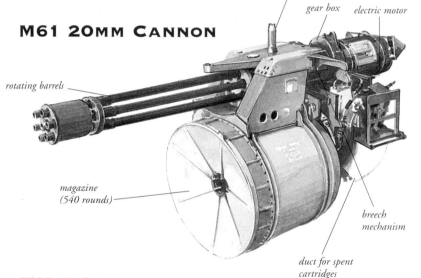

Nose strakes   *Engine air intake*

Low voltage formation lights

M61 20-mm cannon with 540 rounds

'Plugged-in' deck crew talking to pilot

Catapult launch ignition lights

Centerline drop tank, 300 US gallons

Catapult shuttle   *Catapult strop link*

voice communication, it also carries the Link 4A datalink. The F/A-18 can receive UHF (UHF/DF), VHF (Tactical Air Navigation TACAN) and HF Automatic Direction Finding (ADF) beacons as well as Global Position System (GPS) signals for navigation. All this capability is indicated by antennas sprouting over the Hornet.

The cockpit canopy of a single-seat F/A-18C is positioned for all-around visibility (looking aft between the two fins). This is an improvement over 1960s fighter designs, which often neglected the 'Mark I eyeball' and paid dearly for it in air combat over Vietnam.

Most F/A-18s are single seaters. Advanced electronics systems can do most of the work of a back-seater. However, the US Marine Corps makes extensive use of two-seat F/A-18Ds in combat roles, with the back-seaters serving as forward air controllers for other aircraft as well.

For all its complexity, the F/A-18 is noted for ease of maintenance and reliability. For planning purposes in the 1970s, it was usually considered that 60% of a carrier's air wing would be available at any given time; often less. There was widespread criticism that the advanced systems of the F/A-18 would decrease the number available. This has not been the case. F/A-18s on extended deployments average availability rates of over 80%. In the Gulf War an average of 90% of all F/A-18s were mission available, with a peak of 95%, although at that time all the US Navy's resources were devoted to sustaining only half the Hornet force. Nevertheless, the sustained F/A-18 operations over Bosnia have been marked by 93% availability.

The F/A-18 remains more than the sum of all its parts. It is much harder to have multi-

mission aircrew than design a multi-mission aircraft. The US Navy has for a generation — since its embarrassing setbacks over Vietnam – put the emphasis on producing aircrew that can not only defeat any enemy in combat, but survive the harsh environment of flying off an aircraft carrier at sea. Especially in the Cold War years, when North Atlantic and North Pacific operations were stressed, the US Navy trained hard in a way made possible by the defense budgets of the 1980s. Even though the money is now gone, the expertise remains. "It's not the ships, it's the men in them" was a saying of the age of sail; it remains equally true in the age of the microchip.

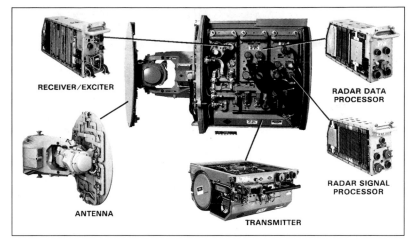

RECEIVER/EXCITER — RADAR DATA PROCESSOR — ANTENNA — TRANSMITTER — RADAR SIGNAL PROCESSOR

The Hughes APG-73 is an advanced version of the APG-65 multi-mode radar (shown here). The later model has programmable digital signal processors for enhanced flexibility in both air-to-air and air-to-surface missions.

Navigation light

ECM antenna

RWR antenna

Low voltage formation lights

elevon pivot

arrestor hook

Moveable leading edge in take-off position

flaps in take-off position

AIM-120A AMRAAM anti-aircraft missile

Main landing gear

John B Ridyard

WARZONE:
F/A-18s OVER THE STRAIT OF HORMUZ

To consider where aircraft such as the F/A-18 may be in action in the future, it is a good idea to look first where they have been in the past. The Strait of Hormuz and the Gulf, which it separates from the Arabian Sea, are never far away from the thoughts of decision-makers and war-fighters alike. F/A-18s became a familiar sight in and around the Gulf in the mid-1980s as the US Navy increased its commitment to keep navigation open during the Iran-Iraq War. Two-thirds of the world's known oil reserves are in lands that border the Gulf. The oil traffic that flows through the Strait of Hormuz is the lifeblood of the developed world. Keeping these waters safe for shipping led to clashes with Iranian forces in which US naval units and carrier-based aircraft sank or crippled several Iranian warships. Navy and Marine F/A-18s and Canadian CF-18s were a vital part of the air campaign in the Gulf War of 1991. Since then, F/A-18s have taken their turn enforcing the no-fly zone over southern Iraq. The F/A-18 is no stranger to the Gulf or to combat.

This particular F/A-18 will be launching today, as will several dozen other US Navy aircraft, with live ordnance. Its pilot, if fortunate, will be entering today's mission in his logbook in the traditional green ink that marks combat time. The reason for this is because, at some time in the future, it is postulated that the Iranians have decided to interfere with tanker traffic sailing through the Strait of Hormuz.

Today, Iran's economy remains dependent on oil for export earnings. The world oil market is shaped by a cartel — OPEC (The Organization of Petroleum Exporting Countries) — that is largely controlled by countries that fear and dislike Iran, most notably the Kingdom of Saudi Arabia (KSA) and the states of the Gulf Coordination Council (GCC). Iran may decide at some time in the future that, though its rivals may control the market, it can control the Straits and so render meaningless oil quotas it sees as unfair or exclusionary.

There are other reasons why Iran may not wish to let its oil disputes with either OPEC or the United States be resolved by the diplomats. The Iranians also have a history of using violence for political ends, from attacks on shipping during the Iran-Iraq war to state support for terrorism in both the Middle East and Europe. Finally, Iran is indeed an evil empire in the sense that Ronald Reagan originally used the term: human rights. This is a government that hangs Baha'is and Jews because of their religious practices.

It is not far-fetched to consider what might happen if Iran were to use military leverage to balance their adversaries' economic advantage. In this scenario, the Iranians have claimed that they will impose their own quotas of tankers which will be allowed through the straits. They are enforcing this with shore-based anti-ship missiles, Chinese-built 'Silkworms' and C-802s. These missiles are being targeted against ships which are being detected by a Chinese-built Iranian gunboat, operating in the strait. There is concern that the Iranians will next try and mine the main channel.

The US carrier battle group — of which this F/A-18 is part of the air wing — had been tasked, at first, with surveillance of the Iranian efforts. This means there have been daily fighter patrols over the area. If the Iranians had started to mine the straits or bring up their Russian-built diesel-powered attack submarines, it might have triggered an immediate response. Now, a new order has been received: destroy the Iranian missiles and the gunboats doing their targeting.

This order will have come down from the national command authority (NCA) of the United States — the man in the White House — after coordination with friends and allies, consideration of diplomatic options, informing Congressional leadership, and the writing of highly classified memoranda by groups ranging from planning staffs to international lawyers. Then once issued, the order for this air strike traveled from the NCA via the Chairman of the Joint Chiefs of Staff (JCS) to Central Command (CENTCOM) to the US Navy's Fifth Fleet command (the naval portion of CENTCOM) to the admiral commanding the carrier battle group.

The procedure is quicker is reality than it sounds and the NCA has, in the past, elected to micro-manage crises directly. In 1988, during a previous battle with the Iranian Navy, the Secretary of Defense in Washington personally gave the order for US carrier aircraft to spare a damaged Iranian frigate. In 1975, an A-7 pilot in mid-mission was put directly in touch with the White House situation room during the *Mayaguez* incident. In other incidents, there is no doubt that US Navy aircraft have been lost because the authorities in Washington have specified such

details as the altitude at which missions must be flown, rather than leaving it to the men on the scene.

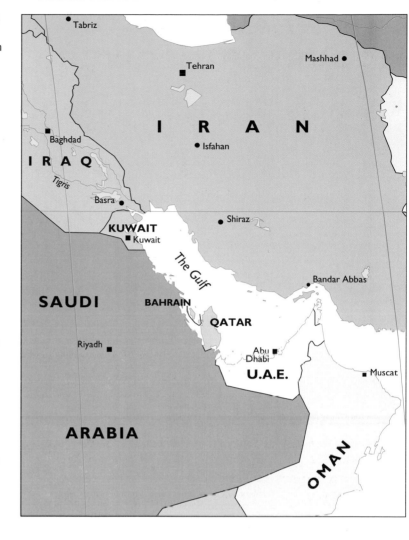

Above: The Gulf carries a large percentage of the world's oil supplies, and its shipping is highly vulnerable to interdiction by missiles and aircraft.

Left: This line-up of carrier air wing CVW-1 Hornets aboard the USS George Washington (CVN-73) represents a mix of F/A-18Cs from VFA-82 'Marauders' and VFA-86 'Sidewinders', both home-based at NAS Cecil Field, Florida.

THE REALITIES OF MODERN AIRPOWER

The F/A-18 and its pilot represent a combination of the "right stuff" — the mixture of aggressiveness, tempered confidence, and skill that made successful fighter pilots in the First and Second World War — with modern technology. The successful fighter pilot has always been a master of airplane, technology, weapons, and tactics alike. Today's F/A-18 pilot has been trained to emulate this model. However, his mission will be much more complicated than those of World War II or even jet-age conflicts such as the Vietnam and Falklands wars. The F/A-18 pilot, in the upcoming mission, will have to accurately deliver a wide range of weapons, both air-air and air-surface. He will have to rely on a greater range of sensors to both carry out his mission and survive an equally capable enemy response.

Above: A Navy F/A-18C from VFA-82 seen during Operation Desert Storm. The aircraft is carrying three 330 US gallon (1,250-litre) tanks, giving a ferry range of more than 2,000 nautical mile. (3,700 km)

THE US NAVY AND THE GULF

The F/A-18's mission is also part, not only of US national policy, but also of the role of the US Navy in the Gulf. The US Navy's involvement in the Gulf and its role in power projecting are both long standing.

The carrier from which the mission will be launched is one of twelve in the US Navy. The use of these carriers has often been the decisive element in the US response to a crisis, even when no shots have been fired. Just as the US is unique in being the world's only superpower, the carriers, their air wings, and their capabilities are also all unique.

There is nothing else like them in other navies.

This upcoming mission will demonstrate one of the carrier's advantages. Unlike bases ashore, there is no international political cost to mounting air strikes from land bases in foreign countries, no requirement for putting a coalition together before military action can be taken. The strike can still be launched even if US friends in the region are not participating in the action against Iran, preferring instead to regret the use of force in public and applaud in private.

Below: A Northrop Grumman A-6E Intruder of VA-85 'Buckeyes', home-based at NAS Oceana, Virginia, is about to leave the USS America, while an F/A-18C from VFA-86 waits its turn for the catapult.

STRIKE PLANNING

Above: Four 1,000 lb (450 kg) Mk83 LDGP (low drag general purpose) bombs are released from an F/A-18D of VMFA(AW)-533 in a medium dive attack.

Strike planning is where the abstract policy considerations of higher levels must be translated into the hard and dangerous realities of air combat operations. Today, the process is increasingly automated, using the TAC-3 (Tactical Advanced Computer), which is being upgraded to the TAMPS (Tactical Air Mission Planning System, the Navy and Marine Corps standard system). The Air Courses of Action Assessment Model (ACAAM) can be used to "wargame out" different strike options before the detailed planning is made. Computerized work stations bring the different factors in mission planning together.

The new technology's advantages include the ability to "fly" a planned mission in a modeled three-dimensional view, with the aircraft shown evading SAMs (Surface-to-Air Missiles), going down valleys and over ridge lines. Alternatively, it can show a "God's eye view" of the entire operation. Weather is automatically incorporated into the automated planning process from the latest reports. Where, in the past, sailors in the intelligence department had to prepare appropriate maps for low-level missions by hand, the system can now produce them with a color printer.

Yet mission planning remains an art rather than a science. Much of the planning is done by the men who will lead and fly the strike.

This way, they can be sure that they are not being sent into harm's way lightly by those who will not be sharing the risks. Squadron commanders will use their expertise to make sure that the capabilities and limitations of their aircraft are reflected in the plan.

Before the details of the strike are worked out, the decision must be made on how to carry it out. Will this require 22 or more aircraft at medium altitude? Or will eight F/A-18s, four with bombs, four to protect against fighters and SAMs, and an EA-6B, all coming in low trying to keep the element of surprise, be sufficient?

Also determining the planning process will be the Rules of Engagement (RoE). This will include which targets are not to be hit, and the conditions under which aircraft can open fire. It will limit the battle group's authority to conduct operations over time and space. Political considerations will be important here as well. This is why, in the upcoming mission, 'Nickel Flight' will be visually identifying their targets rather than despatching them with long-range missiles.

The timing of the mission, from zero hour, must be carefully orchestrated. Because so many different types of aircraft must coordinate with each other and with the ships of the battle group, precise timing is required. The goal will be for the aircraft of the strike to hit their targets in a concentrated mass, overwhelming the defenses.

Modern jet aircraft are thirsty beasts, so fuel is an important determinant of planning. It will dictate the sequence in which aircraft launch, how they refuel from tankers and recover. These considerations will be reflected in rendezvous times, arrival times and waypoints.

Planning must never leave the enemy out of the process. The carrier's (CV in the US Navy abbreviation) intelligence center, the CVIC, provides "one-stop shopping", integrating the information the battle group has from its own sensors with that received from national level and other sensors. The routes to and from the target will be determined by the location of enemy radars, SAMs, and AAA (Anti-Aircraft Artillery). These can be called up on the workstations used for mission planning, with radii drawn around them to show their effective "envelopes" and where such envelopes may be blocked by terrain masking. When possible, friendly aircraft will seek to avoid these envelopes. When they are not able to, planning must provide another counter, in the form of defense suppression.

Weaponeering — matching weapons to targets — is another key part of the planning process. It is important that this part of the mission is carried out by those who will be flying it. The right weapon must be matched to the right target. Weather plays a vital part in the weaponeering process. The basic approach of this strike — medium altitude, using laser-guided bombs (LGBs) — is possible because of the lack of low clouds. Otherwise, an under-the-weather attack with different weapons might be required.

In a mission such as this, even one aircraft lost can be of potentially international significance. Each shot-down crew member can be used as a hostage. Emergency procedures and mission abort procedures will be determined as part of the planning process. The US Navy takes its Combat Search and Rescue (CSAR) capabilities seriously.

For use over voice radio, brevity codes for different elements of the strike, objectives, and threats will be determined. While the F/A-18's UHF has a secure capability using the KY-58 encryption device, for each mission a list of brevity codes is generated and issued to all aircrew participating in the strike. The US Navy has learned that third world opponents are still likely to have lots of trained English-speakers to monitor communications.

Before the mission, the aircrews will be thoroughly briefed, first at an air wing strike brief and then in each squadron ready room, where each squadron will review their part in the operations. Some of the areas will be part of the air wing's standard operating procedures (SOPs). Communication and weather are vital parts of the briefing. Finally, F/A-18 crews will talk about how they will carry out their part of the mission.

The end results of the planning process are

Below: Long-range fleet air defence against aircraft launching stand-off missiles is provided by the Northrop Grumman F-14 Tomcat.

directly applicable to the mission itself. Waypoints along the course to and from the targets are entered into the inertial navigation systems (INS) of F/A-18s. The electronic threat-reference library of the ALR-67 RHAW (Radar Homing and Warning) gear on board each F/A-18 is updated to reflect the latest ELINT (electronic intelligence) information acquired by the ES-3As operating from the carrier. Even the terrain around the targets will be taken into account for setting the F/A-18's radio altimeters prior to dive-bombing attacks.

Below: The variety of aircraft types accommodated by US Navy carriers is illustrated here, with a Hornet sandwiched between a Lockheed Martin S-3A Viking and a Northrop Grumman E-2C Hawkeye.

STRIKE FORCE: THE CARRIER BATTLE GROUP

The aircraft carrier may be the most powerful warship in the world, but it does not go to war by itself. It is a part of an integrated group of ships, the carrier battle group. Each of these ships is there for a specific purpose, to both protect the carrier and join with it at striking at any possible target on land, sea, air, or under water.

The carrier battle group is not just an impressive and incredibly expensive collection of ships, aircraft, and weapons. The US Navy has designed and constructed the different ships and aircraft and trained their crews to fit together into a cohesive, coherent operational concept. Everything is in the battle group to carry out several overlapping missions.

The F/A-18 is just one of these elements. The carrier's fighters are the dual-purpose —

attack and defense — main battery of the battle group. But how they will act is determined in part by other ships and aircraft of the battle group.

The other warships in the battle group make it possible for the carrier air wing to carry out its missions and take part in these missions themselves. These missions have traditionally been dominated by the three basic types of naval warfare: anti-aircraft warfare (AAW), anti-submarine warfare (ASW), and anti-

Above: Another busy deck scene, with Tomcats of VF-33 'Starfighters' and VF-102 'Diamondbacks' (both with self-explanatory squadron markings), and a Northrop Grumman KA-6D tanker of VA-85 in the background.

Left: The 80,800-ton USS John F Kennedy (CV-67), the fourth of the Kitty Hawk class, developed from the earlier Forrestal series. The ship has a maximum speed of 33 knots (61 km/hr) and a range of up to 8,000 nautical miles (14,800 km

surface warfare (ASuW). However, the US Navy has had limited need to carry out these naval missions during the decades of the Cold War and, with the demise of the Soviet Navy, it appears that even less of the battle group's resources will be devoted to these purely naval missions.

Although since the 1950s, the US Navy's carriers have been training to defeat the Soviet Union in a general conflict, they have been frequently used in 'power projection' missions around the world. Sometimes, power is projected by presence alone, either to demonstrate the long-reach of the United States and prevent a crisis from escalating, or to evacuate civilians. On other occasions, the carriers have intervened by sending carrier aircraft to strike ground targets — as was done in Korea, Vietnam, Lebanon in 1983, Libya in 1986, the Gulf War, and Bosnia. In this mission, the F/A-18 is, in attacking an Iranian gunboat, making an anti-surface attack in the context of an overall power projection mission.

CARRIER FLIGHT OPERATIONS

Flight operations from a carrier are inherently complex in a way even beyond those of modern fighter missions from shore bases. No one has ever run an airbase onto the rocks! A carrier may have the operational flexibility to move at 35 miles per hour, but it also has to deal with the realities of keeping the sea.

The operational life of an aircraft carrier revolves around its operations cycle. Each 100-minute time period of the day will have a particular purpose, even when the carrier is not conducting round-the-clock operations. Normally, each cycle is devoted to the launch and recovery of aircraft with the launches being at the start and the recoveries at the end of each cycle. During launch operations, the goal is to bring up aircraft from the hangar deck, position them on the flight deck, and launch them by catapult as soon as possible. This usually results in a crowded flight deck. During landing operations, the priorities are reversed. The flight deck is kept relatively open so that aircraft landing can be taxied out of the way as quickly as possible.

Carrier operations in combat have been dominated by cyclic operations although a recent innovation, the battle flex deck, allows more flexibility and gets away from the cycle. Cyclic operations are how sustained air operations at sea are carried out. As part of cyclic operations in combat, a carrier will launch and recover its combat air patrols (CAPs).

Usually, a carrier facing a potential air threat will keep at least one pair of fighters aloft in a barrier CAP (BARCAP) in the air on the primary threat axis (the direction the enemy is expected to come from). If there is room on the flight deck or if the threat requires it, a BARCAP can be backed up by a "deck CAP" of crewed aircraft on the carrier deck, ready to launch. A target CAP (TARCAP)

covers the strike against air-air threats coming on and off the target.

Radar and ASW aircraft and tankers all go to their stations and, as they are relieved by fresh aircraft, go back to the carriers in accordance with the cycles. Cyclic operations are not only defensive. They can include strike packages, although the number of aircraft sent up is limited only by the carrier's ability to launch or recover during a single cycle. Even a large-scale carrier air strike — such as the one that the F/A-18 is going on — is capable of being launched within the opening 15 minutes or so of a cycle.

Above: US carriers have 4 catapults, giving a high launch rate. Here, an F/A-18C departs from the right-hand catapult on the straight-through deck, while an S-3A prepares to follow from the left unit.

Below: USS Dwight D Eisenhower (CVN-69) in transit through the Suez Canal en route for the Mediterranean

THE SHIPS IN THE CARRIER BATTLE GROUP

The ships in the carrier battle group will not simply be protecting the carrier from enemy action, they will be assisting its air group in carrying out its missions.

Above: The USS Mobile Bay (CG-53) is representative of the 9,100-ton Ticonderoga class of Aegis air defence cruisers. It has a crew of 360 and a range of up to 6,000 nautical miles (11,000 km).

Two Ticonderoga (CG-47) Class Aegis Cruisers

The largest surface warships escorting the carrier are the Aegis cruisers which are the primary surface anti-aircraft warfare (AAW) assets of the battle group. They carry the Aegis system, which integrates their phased-array SPY-1 search and fire control radars with different types of Standard surface-to-air missiles. An Aegis system has the capability to defeat flying targets ranging from an incoming supersonic cruise missile at wavetop level to a ballistic missile dropping down from outer space.

Aegis cruisers have a large magazine capacity. Later ships with vertical launch tubes will carry numbers of Tomahawk Land Attack (TLAM) cruise missiles which will be integrated into air strikes. Thus, like the carrier itself, a system originally designed to prevent the Soviet Navy from contesting control of the sea — the Aegis system was designed to protect carriers against Soviet bombers and cruise missiles — has evolved into a more general-purpose power-projection capability.

Two Arleigh Burke (DDG-51) Class Destroyers

The Arleigh Burkes carry on the classic multi-role destroyer capability, although the smaller Spruance-class destroyers are the ASW specialists. The Arleigh Burke class destroyers, also equipped with the Aegis system, will supplement the cruisers in the AAW mission. They also have an ASW capability and their vertical launch tubes also carry TLAM and Harpoon anti-ship missiles.

AIRPOWER AND SEAPOWER

All of the battle group's missions are carried out by both aircraft and ships working together. Because ships and submarines are increasingly equipped with long-range missiles, even over-the-horizon operations are no longer unique to air warfare.

Anti-Air Warfare (Aaw)

When the Soviet Navy was the main challenge to the control of the sea, the US Navy invested much money and thought in winning the air battle. The composition of the battle group shows the investment in AAW made during the Cold War, in the number of fighters, the Standard SM-2-ER SAMs in the vertical launch tubes on the Aegis cruisers and Arleigh Burke destroyers, and the self-defense NATO Sea Sparrow missiles and

Two Spruance (DD-963) Class Destroyers

The Spruance destroyers are the battle group's primary surface anti-submarine warfare assets. They will often embark an SH-60B LAMPS III helicopter on their fantail. These destroyers carry the NATO Sea Sparrow SAM for self-defense against aircraft. They are often used to cover replenishment ships sustaining the battle group at sea and as plane-guard destroyers (accompanying the carrier during flight operations and using its helicopter to pick up any aircrew who have been forced to eject on landing or launch).

Two Los Angeles (SSN-688) Class Attack Submarines

The Los Angeles class submarine is the battle group's ASW specialist. Unlike other nuclear attack submarines, it was designed from the keel up to work with the fast carriers, sacrificing some quietness for sustained high cruising speed. It will be stationed on the primary threat axis for enemy submarines, usually some 60-70 nautical miles away from the carrier. In this case, surface and air ASW platforms will be put on a "weapons tight" status in these areas.

While designed to protect the carriers from Soviet submarines, since the end of the Cold War, these boats have been given new capabilities. SSN-688s also attack surface

ships with Harpoon missiles and targets ashore with TLAMs. The SSNs can also collect ELINT (electronic intelligence) by raising an antenna while at periscope depth.

One Supply Class Replenishment Ship

Replenishment makes the whole battle group operation possible. The US Navy keeps the sea, which means that its warships require constant UNREPS (underway replenishments) of fuel, bombs, food, and anything else. These fast replenishment ships are intended to operate with the carrier battle groups without reducing their operational tempo.

Above: The 7,800-ton Spruance class of anti-submarine destroyers have a crew of 302 and a range of up to 6,000 nautical miles (11,000 km). This is USS Caron (DD-970).

Phalanx gun systems on the other ships.

Incoming bombers and cruise missiles would have had to fight their way through a multi-layered defense coordinated by radar from E-2Cs and ships. F-14 CAPs, a "missile trap" of an Aegis ship (a role being played in this mission by the forward deployed Aegis cruiser), the carrier's inner and outer escort screen and closer-in F/A-18 CAPs. This required highly evolved IFF (Identification Friend or Foe) techniques to integrate fighters and Standard SAMs.

Left: The E-2C is the Navy's AWACS, but its target acquisition range is limited by the turboprop's lower cruise altitude.

Right: An F-14 of VF-33 'Starfighters' waits behind the protection of the jet blast deflector for an F/A-18C to depart the right-hand catapult.

ANTI-SUBMARINE WARFARE (ASW)

Like AAW, the carrier battle group would fight both an inner and outer battle, although in this case the range would be determined by the location of sound convergence zones and thermal layers in the ocean: sea conditions that largely determine how far sonars can detect submarines.

Far right: USS Newport News (SSN-750), one of the 6,900-ton Los Angeles class of nuclear-powered hunter-killer submarines.

In the outer battle, the SSN-688s and S-3s from the carrier, in conjunction with shore-based P-3Cs would keep the threats away from the carrier. If a threat penetrated toward the carrier, the inner ASW battle would be waged by SH-60F helicopters from the carrier, SH-60B helicopters from the escorts and by the escorts themselves. The longest range surface ASW weapon, the ASROC, which is a rocket-boosted anti-submarine torpedo, was limited by the convergence zone range of the ship's sonar, but the submarines, under the thermal layer, could use the Mk 48 homing torpedo for long-range kills.

Since the early 1970s, submarines have had the ability to fire anti-ship missiles at the carrier while submerged. Thus, a submarine threat can turn into an air threat instantly and fighter CAPs must often be involved in the prosecution of a submarine contact.

POWER PROJECTION AND AMPHIBIOUS OPERATIONS

Below: The Lockheed Martin S-3 Viking is the US Navy's standard carrier-borne ASW aircraft. Variants include the ES-3A electronic intelligence aircraft and the US-3A carrier onboard delivery aircraft.

The Navy's primary tool for power projection is the carrier's air wing. In the Gulf War, the sixteen-inch guns of the battleships contributed to this mission, but today the Navy relies on the Tomahawk Land Attack Missiles (TLAMs) carried by the Aegis cruisers, Arleigh Burke destroyers, and SSN-688 submarines to work synergistically with the aircraft.

Replenishment

Aircraft also contribute to the replenishment mission. High-priority cargo (such as mail) and personnel are flown onto the carrier in a COD (carrier on-board delivery) aircraft like the Grumman C-2 Greyhound. Replenishment ships use on-board CH-46 helicopters to lift priority deliveries to the ships of the battle group, winching them down onto destroyers too small for the twin-engine CH-46 to come aboard.

More Power For The Battle Group

To carry out its mission of removing the Iranian threats to traffic through the Strait of Hormuz, the battle group will have support from assets that are not under command of its rear admiral.

TENCAP assets

The TENCAP (tactical exploitation of national capabilities) program dates from the late 1970s. It aimed to make the increasing array of sensor platforms intended to support the US national command authority available to theaters of operations in a timely manner. This includes data from satellites (photo, ELINT, and radar) and aircraft such as U-2Rs.

Space-based assets

The carrier battle group is dependent on satellite communications for most of its long-range command and control. Infrared satellite warning of ballistic missile launches — which proved vital for defense against Scud missiles during the Gulf War — can also be provided to theater commanders through the Navy's Radiant Ivory system.

EP-3E Aries ELINT aircraft

These large, shore-based ELINT aircraft, modified versions of the standard ASW aircraft, monitor enemy radars and communications. They can either respond to high-level taskings from the national command authorities or be 'chopped' to support the battleground.

P-3C ASW aircraft

The Navy's first-line sub-hunter aircraft can use its long range to support carrier operations in most potential trouble spots. Its excellent communications, surface search radar, and infrared sensor make it highly valuable in a broad spectrum of operations.

ROTHR

The ROTHR (Relocatable Over The Horizon Radar) may provide the battle group with additional situational awareness, detecting threats at long range by bouncing its signals off the ionosphere. A ROTHR located on Diego Garcia in the Indian Ocean could support operations in the Arabian Sea.

The USAF

The US Air Force could also support the battle group. Most significantly, modified KC-135 and KC-10 tankers can provide in-flight refueling, RC-135 Rivet Joints can supplement EP-3Es in the ELINT mission. Naval TLAM attacks can be supplemented by long-range B-52Hs firing Conventional Air-Launched Cruise Missiles (CALCMs). During the Cold War, B-52s trained in anti-ship attacks with Harpoon missiles and long-range minelaying.

Below: The Lockheed Martin P-3C Orion is the Navy's standard land-based maritime patrol and ASW aircraft. This one is from VP-31 'Black Lightnings', based at NAS Moffett Field, California.

THE CARRIER AIR WING

The F/A-18 is not going to war alone. It will do so as part of a airstrike with all the different types of aircraft on the carrier participating and supported by missiles from the battle group's surface warships. The organization that will integrate the different squadrons is the carrier air wing.

Above: Deck congestion is such that aircraft are routinely parked overhanging the edge of the deck, as in the case of these F/A-18Cs, S-3 and A-6Es.

The "CAG" (from the old-style name of his command, the carrier air group), the commander of the carrier air wing, is a naval captain, generally one being groomed for potential command of a carrier. He is responsible to the ship's captain, administratively and operationally to the rear admiral commanding the battle group. Under the CAG is the air wing staff, which handles administration, intelligence, planning, and logistics and support.

The composition of US Navy carrier air wings is changing in the post Cold War world. Most wings will consist of three fighter squadrons: one with 14 F-14s and two with 18 F/A-18s each. Vital radar and electronic warfare functions will be handled by a squadron each of four-five E-2Cs and three-six EA-6Bs. Where there is not a full squadron in the wing, it may be reinforced by a detachment of a type of aircraft required by the mission.

THE AIRCRAFT OF THE AIR WING

Grumman F-14D Tomcat fighter

The swing-wing fighter was designed to defend the fleet, using its long-range Phoenix missiles to destroy incoming bombers and cruise missiles. Since the end of the Cold War removed the most severe air threats, F-14s have also gotten into the air-ground business as well, and have been used in this role in Bosnia.

Lockheed S-3B Viking ASW aircraft

The eight-ten S-3Bs are the carrier air wing's primary platform for the outer ASW battle. When not engaged in ASW, S-3s carry out ASuW missions using their excellent ALR-67 ESM (electronic support measures, another designation for passive sensors), APS-137 inverse synthetic aperture (ISAR) surface-search radars and Harpoon missiles. In the Gulf War, S-3s bombed Iraqi ground targets. They can also carry out buddy-tanking missions.

Grumman E-2C Hawkeye airborne early warning aircraft

A radar's range is longer if its antenna is higher. Without the E-2C, the battle group would be limited to the radar horizon from the top of each ship's masthead. The E-2C's APS-145 UHF-band radar has been upgraded to give it better capability against overland targets. The ALR-73 Passive Detection System (PDS) is used in conjunction with the radar to identify contacts. The E-2C's Link 4A, Link 11, and Link 16 datalink systems allow it to mesh information received from the carrier and from other aircraft. A carrier air wing will normally keep one of its four or five E-2Cs airborne at all times when in action.

Grumman EA-6B Prowler electronic warfare aircraft

Another vital high-technology force multiplier, the three-six EA-6Bs of the air wing detect enemy radars using ESM (electronic support measures) equipment. An EA-6B can then either try and destroy the radar with a Highspeed Anti-Radiation Missile (HARM) or jam it with its ALQ-99 jammers.

Grumman A-6E Intruder attack aircraft and KA-6D tanker

A carrier air wing can count itself lucky if it has a detachment of A-6s or four KA-6Ds. This veteran all-weather attack aircraft is leaving service and will not be deploying regularly after fiscal year 1997. However, its large payload makes it an excellent tanker aircraft and at the end of its career the A-6 has frequently carried out this mission.

Lockheed ES-3A Shadow electronic intelligence aircraft

Not an integral part of the air wing, detachments of one or two ES-3s will deploy aboard a carrier to provide the battle group with highly capable ELINT available in near real-time.

Sikorsky SH-60F ASW helicopter

Operating from the carrier, the six or eight helicopters of this type are capable of using dipping sonar to prosecute submarine contacts, then attacking with homing torpedoes. The crews of these helicopters are trained in both ASW and strike rescue tactics. The earlier SH-60B LAMPS III version operates from cruisers and destroyers, though both this and the SH-60H will be upgraded to the SH-60R version starting in the late 1990s.

Sikorsky HH-60H rescue helicopter

Detachments of Navy HH-60H rescue and special operations helicopters are often deployed as part of an air wing. The HH-60Hs are specialists in penetrating enemy airspace if required, and can be forward deployed on a destroyer or cruiser fantail to be closer to the action. While the Navy currently lacks a long-range combat search and rescue aircraft, aircrew rescue around the battle group is carried out by SH-60s. An SH-60 will normally fly plane-guard duties close to a carrier whenever air operations are underway.

Grumman C-2 Greyhound

The cargo version of the E-2C is found in detachments in deployed battle groups and at supporting shore bases world wide. It flies priority cargo and personnel to the carrier and also has a combat role, inserting special operations forces.

OTHER CARRIERS, OTHER MISSIONS

Britain's 19,500-ton HMS Invincible was the first of its class and played a major role in the Falklands war.

The size of US Navy carriers and the amount of money invested in their aircraft gives them capabilities far greater than any other comparable ship. The Royal Navy's three 'through-deck cruisers' (a euphemism chosen to escape sidestep political opposition to building carriers) each have an air group of up to eight Sea Harrier FRAS.2 fighter-bombers, nine Sea King ASW helicopters, and three Sea King AEW.2 radar helicopters. While the new French nuclear carrier *Charles de Gaulle* will have an airgroup including the naval version of the Rafale fighter and E-2Cs, the current French carriers must continue to use geriatric F-8E(FN) Crusaders. The air-ground mission (and, realistically, much of the air-air as well) is carried out by 15-19 Super Etendards and eight Alize turboprops. A US carrier can offer not only the quality of operational sophistication due to investment in greater numbers and types of aircraft, it also has the advantage in pure weight of firepower.

Above: France's nuclear-powered Charles de Gaulle is due to be commissioned in mid-1999.

FLIGHT CREWS:
THE F/A-18 PILOT

The F/A-18 pilot is the one indispensable element of mission equipment. The F/A-18 pilot's equipment is, like the aircraft itself, state of the art. It is intended to let a single pilot do the work that once required a crew of two in the F-4 Phantom, which the F/A-18 replaced on the Navy's carriers. However, the most dangerous part of the entire F/A-18 is also the pilot. Flying from an aircraft carrier remains a risky business, even in peacetime, and misjudgment and human failure still has the potential to totally negate the remaining capabilities of the aircraft. Carrier operations are still terribly unforgiving.

The F/A-18 pilot is, like the aircraft, a transitional figure. Some of his equipment represents an improvement over that used in earlier fighters, while much remains the same. He lacks some of the latest innovations, such as a helmet-mounted sight which, slaved to air-to-air missiles, makes sure the missiles are pointed in the same direction as the pilot is looking.

In addition to the equipment shown here, the F/A-18 pilot could carry additional specialized equipment if a mission demanded it. For example, night-vision goggles could be used for a mission requiring low-level visual identification at night. These were extensively used by USMC F/A-18Ds during the Gulf War. It is in these situations that the second pair of eyes provided by a back-seater are most useful.

Left: The complexity of the gear worn by a modern combat aircraft aircrew is shown by this portrait of a Marine Hornet pilot. The tinted visor may provide some protection against lasers, but further development is required.

Left: Wearing his bone-dome, immersion suit, g-suit, flying overalls and life-vest, this pilot has some of the best protection that modern technology can provide. The rest of his survival gear is carried by the ejection seat.

THE EJECTOR SEAT

Even if the F/A-18 pilot does not succeed, he can always leave in style. He sits on a state-of-the-art "bang seat", the SJU-5/6. Like the aircraft itself, it represents an order of magnitude improvement over the previous generation in service. For a naval fighter, "zero-zero" capability is especially important. This means that the pilot can eject even if the aircraft has zero airspeed and is at zero feet altitude. One of the most feared possibilities a carrier pilot can encounter is a "cold launch". This is when a steam catapult fails to deliver the necessary force to bring the aircraft up to flying speed. Sometimes, the shock of a catapult launch will cause an engine to flame out.

Below: An F/A-18D from VMFA(AW)-121 prepares for take off at NAS Miramar.

In either event, the result can be the same: an airplane plunging into the water immediately in front of an 80,000 ton ship moving at almost forty miles an hour. This means that the pilot has a very narrow window of opportunity to realize the problem and then eject. The SJU-5/6 ejection seat keeps this window as large as possible.

Other times a pilot may need to use an ejection seat when the F/A-18 is not even moving. Pilots have ejected on carrier decks when the bombs on the aircraft next to them have prematurely detonated. Ejection has been required before the engines have started, when aircraft have slid off pitching carriers in high seas, taking their pilots with

Drogue
parachute
deployment
gun

Pitot

Canopy breaker

Visor

Main
parachute
container

Electronic
sequencer

Shoulder
harness
restraint
mechanism

Manual
operation
handle

Seat pan

Rocket
motors

SJU—5/A EJECTOR SEAT

Martin-Baker have been making ejector seats for 40 years, and the F/A-18's microprocessor-controlled ejector seat builds on this experience. Seat controls and geometry features are positioned for easy access and the narrowed upper seat bucket allows unrestricted access to side console controls. The headrest is relatively narrow and the seat allows enough freedom of movement not to restrict the pilot's field of vision.

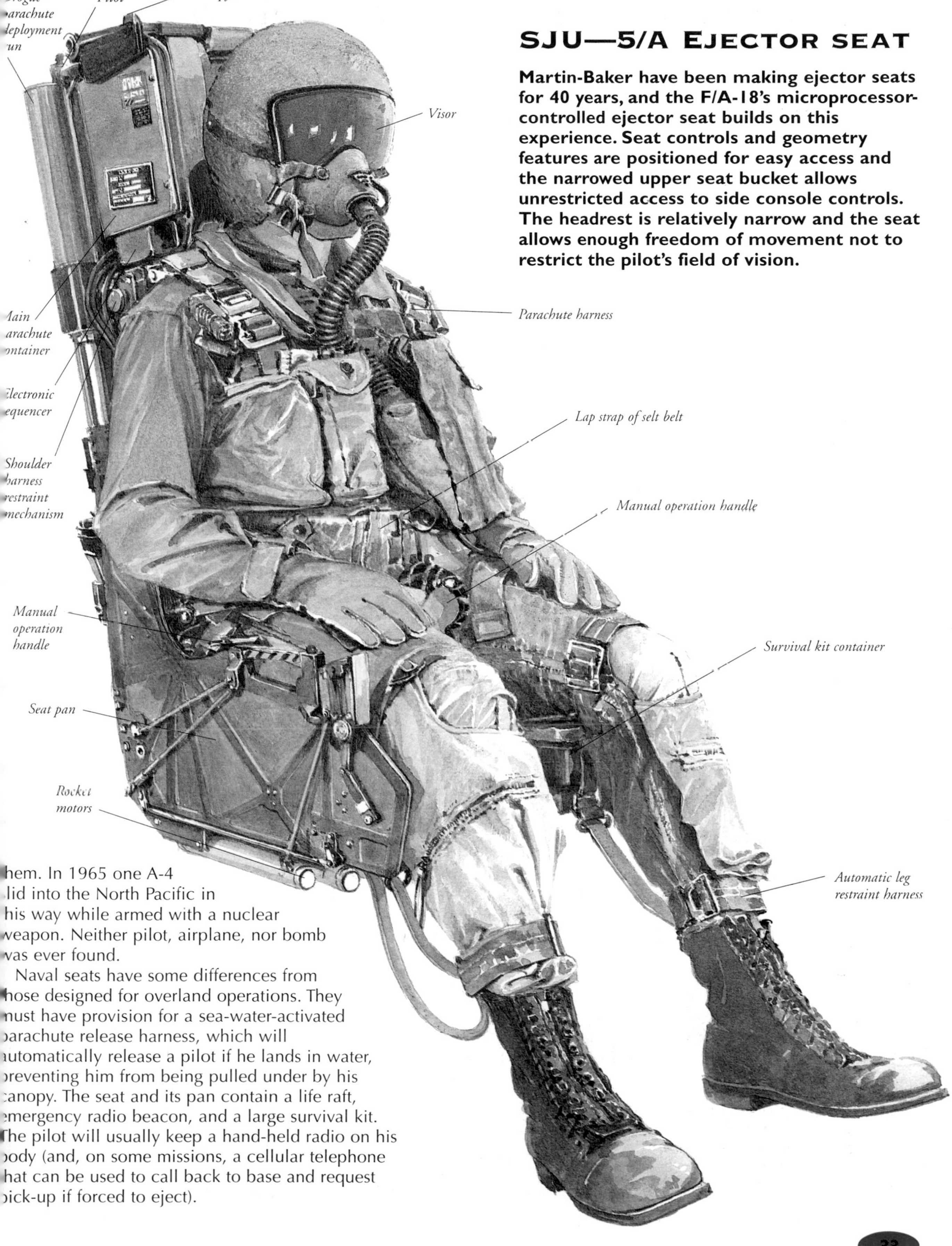

Parachute harness

Lap strap of selt belt

Manual operation handle

Survival kit container

Automatic leg
restraint harness

hem. In 1965 one A-4 lid into the North Pacific in his way while armed with a nuclear weapon. Neither pilot, airplane, nor bomb was ever found.

Naval seats have some differences from hose designed for overland operations. They must have provision for a sea-water-activated parachute release harness, which will automatically release a pilot if he lands in water, preventing him from being pulled under by his canopy. The seat and its pan contain a life raft, emergency radio beacon, and a large survival kit. The pilot will usually keep a hand-held radio on his body (and, on some missions, a cellular telephone that can be used to call back to base and request pick-up if forced to eject).

THE HORNET CREW

The F/A-18 pilot is going on the mission because he survived the two-and-a-half-year process that is required to put him into the status of a "nugget" pilot, a first-cruise newcomer at the bottom of the carrier air wing's food chain. He then evolved to become a proficient fighter pilot, leading a two-ship section.

The F/A-18 pilot — Navy or Marine Corps — will first learn to be an officer at the US Naval Academy at Annapolis, Naval Reserve Officer Training Corps (NROTC) programs at universities, or Aviation Officer Training School before reporting to Aviation Pre-Flight Indoctrination. Trainees are not spared the rigors of a 6 to 14 week program with extensive drill and a kabuki of ritualized harassment and degradation lovingly administered by USMC NCOs alternating with aviation theory.

Once they have completed this stage, the serious flying begins. At Primary Flight Training, 22 weeks with 67 flight and 27 simulator hours on turboprop T-34C trainers (to be replaced by turboprop JPATS trainers in the future), the pilot learns the basics of how to be a military pilot at Pensacola, Florida or Corpus Christi, Texas.

After primary training, the Navy — unlike the Air Force — divides its incoming pilots into different streams. In the 23 weeks of intermediate flight-training at Kingsville, Texas or Meridian, Mississippi, the F/A-18 pilot will have been introduced to pure jets in the form of T-2Cs (eventually to be replaced by T-45s). He will also start the most challenging part of the whole process, carrier qualification, doing four landings. All Navy pilots are also IFR (Instrument Flight Rules) qualified before graduating pilot training.

Advanced flight training is conducted in TA-4Js, which are being replaced by an integrated trainer-and-simulator system featuring the T-45. The pilot will finish his carrier qualifications with a further six landings — a total of ten full-stop and four touch-and-go landings — and become night qualified. He will also learn to use the wide range of weapons that the F/A-18 will carry into action.

Finally, the pilot gets his coveted gold US Navy pilot's wings. He then goes on to a Fleet Replacement Squadron (still usually referred to by its earlier designation of Replacement Air Group) to learn to fly the two-seat version of the F/A-18 before joining his first squadron. It is only at this point that Marine Corps F/A-18 pilots separate out from the stream to learn the specialties of their mission, with additional training in close air support and cooperation with ground forces.

Despite this expensive training, the Navy considers that first tour "nugget" pilots, who may show up at operational units with some 350 hours total in their logbooks, lack the operational capabilities of their more

Two-seat Hornets are used for various types of training. This Canadian CF-188B is carrying an instrumentation pod on the wingtip, for use on an ACMI (air combat maneuvering instrumentation) range. Note the identification light on the fuselage side, and the fake cockpit painted on the belly.

Above: 'Sumo' and 'Popeye' prepare for take-off in this F/A-18D of VMFA(AW)-121 'Green Knights' based at NAS Miramar.

Right: An 'enemy' airfield created for an exercise with old airframes.

experienced comrades. They will undergo additional training and review, especially concentrating on the most challenging part of the naval aviator's job: night carrier landings. They will also receive the semi-official nickname with which all US Navy and Marine Corps pilots are blessed, which can be used as a radio call sign. They will have the benefit of the constant evaluation of other aircraft's landings and the team spirit of an operational squadron, with its own nickname and traditions dating back to the Cold War, the Second World War or before that. Even in low visibility, gray-on-gray color schemes, Navy aircraft still sport elaborate squadron markings (with two aircraft per squadron now having dispensation for colored versions in peacetime).

There are many different ways of producing a world-class pilot, but the end product tends to be interchangeable. F/A-18 pilots on exchange tours with Canadian and Australian units or (flying other types of aircraft) with the USAF and RAF tend to fit in with no more difficulty than moving to another unit in their own service.

THE FLIGHT DECK CREW

Above: Lined up on their respective catapults, these F/A-18Cs represent VFA-82 (foreground) and VFA-86 (rear). The ladder folds neatly into the underside of the leading edge root extension.

The blue-jersey plane handlers are responsible for the aircraft on deck. They attach the chains on both the flight deck and the hangar deck. When a carrier hits heavy seas, an aircraft breaking lose on a crowded hangar deck can do more damage than a bomb. The blue-jersey men have to prevent this. They also run plane tractors and carry out the whole range of intricate maneuvers required to put aircraft in their correct "spots" on deck.

The 'grapes', in their purple jerseys, are the fuel handlers. They are responsible for fueling the aircraft and maintaining the carrier's fuel supply. This can be carried out either on the hangar deck or the flight deck. Often, as in the case of F/A-18s on "deck CAP", waiting on the catapult for an order to launch, they have their hoses running into the airplanes as their engines are turning over.

The yellow shirts are the plane directors that keep the aircraft under their control when moving on the flight deck. When the F/A-18 starts to taxi on the flight deck, it will be passed from one yellow shirt to the next. No aircraft moves under its own power on the flight deck without a yellow shirt directing it.

The green shirts make sure each aircraft is attached to the catapult before launch, installing the hold-back bar after the pilot has rogered the weight board to make sure that the catapult is set for the proper weight. Other green shirts make sure that the arresting gear is set for the proper weight for each landing aircraft.

The ordnancemen both from the air wing and the carrier crew — wear red jerseys. They will load the weapons aboard the F/A-18 and, as it awaits its turn to catapult launch, they will arm the weapons.

White jerseys are safety personnel. A checked jersey denotes a checker, who inspects aircraft ready for take-off. Those in white jerseys with big red crosses are self-explanatory. They stand ready to deal with the inevitable accidents on the carrier flight deck. Firefighters stand ready in their reflective-silver protective suits.

Like the F/A-18 pilot, if any of these crewmen fail in their tasks, they can die and the carrier can be put out of action. In the 1960s and 1970s there were numerous examples of human failure causing disastrous carrier fires and long casualty lists. Even in peacetime, carrier operations are a deadly serious game.

The F/A-18 mission would not be possible without the flight deck crew. Each is recognizable by their color-coded jerseys.

The brown-jersey plane captain is responsible for making sure the F/A-18 is mission-ready at the time it is required to take off. It is his airplane. He just lets a pilot use it for a mission each day. Like the pilot and unlike most of the flight deck crew, he belongs to the squadron, which is part of the carrier's air wing, not part of the carrier's crew.

Above: A pair of Navy Hornets, in this case representing VFA-113 'Stingers' (the 300 Modex indicating the boss-man's aircraft) and VFA-25 'Fist of the Fleet', both home-based at NAS Leemore, California.

Left: The 'green jackets' of USS America prepare this VFA-86 F/A-18C for take-off, attaching its tow-bar and hold-back. Note the strong diagonal member that transmits the catapult load into the airframe.

CHANGES IN HORNETLAND

In the years since the end of the Cold War, there have been many changes in how F/A-18s are used. F/A-18C/D Hornets have replaced the earlier F/A-18A/Bs in US Navy and Marine Corps active force structure squadrons. The F/A-18C/D features the upgraded APG-73 radar which offers capabilities comparable to the USAF's F-15E's APG-70 radar for all-weather attack missions. The APG-73 allowed the Navy and Marine Corps to start replacing the A-6E Intruder with the F/A-18C/D for all-weather attack.

The focus of the mission for which the F/A-18s train has changed as well. During the Cold War, the focus for training and doctrine was the need to defend carriers against the Soviet Navy, while striking back at threats on the periphery of NATO or Pacific allies. Today, a more general goal of projecting power inland from the sea has taken first priority. With US control of the sea uncontested, the US Navy's F/A-18s are now more concerned with striking targets ashore. The Soviet menace is all but extinct, but new potential enemies — Iranians, North Koreans, Iraqis, Bosnian Serbs — all with access to high-technology weapons on the world market have become the primary threat.

Right: Hook down, this F/A-18C of VFA-82 comes over the stern of the USS America. If the hook fails to engage any of the wires, an angled deck and afterburners will facilitate overshoot.

"STRIKE" AND OTHER TRAINING

The Navy and Marine Corps have honed the edge of their Hornets at "Strike", the nickname of the Naval Strike Warfare Center at NAS Fallon, California. Established in the mid-1980s, it was an attempt to make the optimal use of emerging naval capabilities and to prevent setbacks such as the 1983 attack on Syrian targets.

"Strike" has led to improved operations and tactics that have had contributed to F/A-18 operations in the Gulf War and Bosnia. During the Gulf War, instructors from "Strike" were deployed to UN headquarters to add their expertise to mission planning. The training at "Strike" has reflected the post Cold War priorities. In the past, training emphasized smaller, low-level penetration against ultra-modern Soviet defenses. The focus is now on the type of tactics that would be used against Iran or Iraq.

The carrier air wing flying this hypothetical strike would have spent three weeks of intense training at Fallon before joining the carrier to deploy to the Arabian Sea. The Navy aims to rotate every air wing through Fallon on an 18-month cycle. They are briefed on changes in threat equipment and tactics, on current US tactics, and they fly in tactical conditions, starting with two-ship missions and rapidly becoming more sophisticated. Large-scale strikes involving the entire air wing, as this one here, are the graduation exercise. The Tactical Aircrew Combat

Training System (TACTS) range at Fallon provides a state-of-the-art instrumented range for both air-air and air-surface combat.

In addition to "Strike", the Navy participates in the Red and Green Flag series of exercises at Nellis Air Force Base, in Nevada. Before deploying, the F/A-18's squadron will have had the chance to do a two-week Strike Fighter Air Combat Maneuvering Readiness Program. Starting with section (two-ship) then division (four-ship) tactics, the squadron will go through a wide range of scenarios, including working with E-2C aircraft in both voice- and datalink-guided intercepts. The Attack Advanced Readiness Program (AARP), which used to work with the A-6E force, now trains F/A-18 squadrons in both low- and medium-level attacks.

The aim of these exercises was to get the F/A-18 able to operate in either the air-air or air-surface missions, day or night, with E-2 support or autonomously, all with equally high skill. The F/A-18's multi-mission capability and unmatched range of weapons means that its pilots must be proficient in more different weapons skills than any other fighter pilots flying today.

Left: An F/A-18D of VMFA(AW)-224 prepare to depart MCAS Beaufort. Note the camouflaged helmet covers used by Marine aircrew to eliminate glint.

RESERVES AND MARINES COME TO THE CARRIERS

As the Navy has reduced its force structure, it has compensated by bringing reserve and Marine F/A-18 squadrons onto carriers on a regular basis. One of the Navy's carrier air wings and one Marine Air Wing are all-reserve units. US reserve air units tend to be made up almost exclusively of experienced aircrew that have served with the active forces in the past. Unlike an active force squadron they are unlikely to have a number of first-cruise "nuggets".

The four Navy reserve F/A-18 squadrons are now supplied with almost the same equipment as active squadrons. With the end of the Cold War and the reduction of the Navy's force structure, aircraft and equipment ordered for a larger force were then available

for transfer down to the reserves.

The Marine F/A-18s have the primary responsibility of supporting Marines on the ground. However, as their pilots are all qualified in carrier operations, they have now been tasked increasingly to cruise on Navy carriers, used interchangeably with Navy F/A-18s.

The F/A-18 has proven to be an excellent aircraft for reservists. It is the same aircraft as is used in the active force structure, which makes it easily deployable. The F/A-18 is a forgiving airplane, relatively easy to fly, so reservists do not have to use their flying hours keeping current on the aircraft, but can rather devote them to increasing effectiveness.

Below: This F/A-18A of VMFA-451 'Warlords' carries unusually high-visibility markings. The squadron, based at MCAS Beaufort, is part of MAG-31 and transitioned to the Hornet from the F-4 Phantom in 1987.

WOMEN IN HORNETLAND

Throughout the Cold War, F/A-18 operations were an all-male preserve. Since then, women have become an integral part of them, both as aircrew and plane crew. The first female Hornet pilot was a Canadian — Captain Kim Reid — but there are now several women flying US Navy F/A-18s. With the opening up of jobs on board carriers, more women are now also represented on F/A-18 plane crews in the US Navy. The cockpit of an F/A-18 is now an equal opportunity workplace.

Some of the changes in Hornetland have come as a result of the infamous Tailhook Incident of 1991, when a number of naval officers at the annual convention of a civilian naval aviation association were accused of riotous behavior, including harassing and manhandling female attendees, both civilians and naval officers.

Occurring just after the Gulf War, this incident was seized upon by political opponents of the Navy to counter the favorable image of the service from this conflict. Compounded by several botched investigations, the careers of numerous senior naval aviators were ruined. The Tailhook affair has cost the Navy no less than 32 admirals, more than have been lost at sea in all of America's wars combined! Junior officers were made aware that they could expect no support from the chain of command if charged with (or even remotely and indirectly associated with) such conduct.

While making all the Navy aware of the evils of sexual harassment, the legacy of Tailhook has also made sure that naval aviator's riotous on-shore parties have faded into history alongside those other great naval traditions like rum, the lash and another activity now keenly endorsed by the 'politically correct'.

Above: Women aircrew pose special problems to the Navy, requiring increased seat travel and a less powerful ejection. Current ejector seats are designed for male pilots weighing 135-212 lb (61.3-96.3 kg), but future seats will also have to suit women of only 100-116 lb (45.4-52.7 kg).

WEAPONS:
ARMED AND READY

The F/A-18 carries the broadest range of weapons of any modern combat aircraft. This reflects its dual air-to-air and air-to-ground roles and the specialized weapons required by a naval aircraft. US Navy and Marine Corps F/A-18s have access to some of the most advanced weapons technology available anywhere.

The weapons on each aircraft launched from the carrier will be determined as part of the pre-mission planning. In addition to the built-in M61A1 Vulcan 20mm cannon, a close range weapon of last resort, the F/A-18 will carry two each of two types of air-to-air missile (AAM), heat-seeking AIM-9 Sidewinders for use against targets within visual range — those seen by the pilot — and radar-homing AIM-120 AMRAAM (Advanced Medium Range AAM) missiles that can be used beyond visual range (BVR) at targets detected by radar or infrared sensors.

Most of the F/A-18's business is air to surface. It can carry the full range of US bombs, both unitary and cluster bomb units, either unguided "iron" bombs, or those capable of using laser guidance ("smart bombs"). In the future, the "iron" bombs will be smartened up with GPS guidance.

The laser-guided bombs on board for this mission are relative newcomers to the F/A-18. In the Gulf War, the Navy relied on A-6s for LGB delivery, using its stabilized laser and self-designation capability. As the A-6 is now on its way out of service, the LGB delivery mission shifted to the F/A-18.

The GBU-12B, the Paveway II guided version of the standard Mk 82 500-lb bomb, benefits from that weapon's long, slender, aerodynamically shaped profile. It "flies" better than the GBU-16, even if it lacks its punch. In the strike package of this mission, those F/A-18s tasked with going after the Silkworm missiles on their launchers will be armed with GBU-12. The GBU-24A/B, the LGB version of the standard Mk 84 2,000-pound bomb, uses a Paveway III system for guidance, the and is the standard "bunker buster" of US military airpower. The Paveway II seeker head on the GBU-16s is older technology that the Paveway III or IV system. However, as weather permits this mission to be flown from medium altitude, there is no need for the low-altitude capability that is the main advantage of the later types.

An LGB is dropped as a ballistic weapon,

Above: The Mk80 series of general purpose bombs, based on Douglas aerodynamic developments in 1946, still forms the core of USN/USMC ordnance. Here a Marine of VMFA(AW)-224 adjusts the sway-bracing on an F/A-18D store.

Laser designator

following the course established by the dropping aircraft. This is why an accurate dive-bombing attack maximizes LGB accuracy, although level flight and dive-toss attacks are also used. High altitude release allows the LGB to build up velocity. The LGB enters the transition phase of its trajectory as its seeker head attempts to align its velocity vector (flight path) with the direct line-of-sight to the target. In terminal guidance, the LGB keeps its velocity vector aligned with instantaneous line-of-sight. The instant the LGB is aligned, the reflected laser energy centers on its guidance detector. The guidance then commands the guidance fins to a trail position and the LGB falls on the target ballistically.

In addition to the standard LGBs, F/A-18s can use the AGM-123 Skipper, a powered version of the GBU-16 and the Walleye, an older generation guided bomb.

The iron bombs remain an important element of the F/A-18's armament. One reason the Navy did not initially emphasize giving the F/A-18 a LGB delivery capability is that its iron bomb delivery was highly accurate. This was because of the reliable and precise radar. Once locked onto a target it provides input to the bomb release computer. The computer projects a Continuously Computed Impact Point (CCIP) on the HUD, showing the spot where the bombs would land if the pilot pushed the release button on top of the Hands On Throttle and Stick

Above: The AGM-62 Walleye TV-guided missile developed into the Hughes Walleye II ER/DL (shown here on an F/A-18D) with larger wings and an imaging-infrared seeker.

LOADED

As the A-6E is phased out, the task of delivering laser-guided bombs is shifting to the F/A-18. This Hornet carries two GBU-16 Paveway IIs, plus a centerline tank, two Texas Instruments AGM-88 HARMs (High-speed Anti-Radiation Missiles) for defence-suppression, and two AIM-9s for self-defence.

AIM-9L all-angle heat-seeking anti-aircraft missile

AGM-88 HARM anti-radar missile

Drop tank

AIM-120 AMRAAM anti-aircraft missile

1,000-lb Mk83 GBU-16 B/B Paveway laser-guided bomb

WEAPONS

Above: A clutch of Mk80 bombs, waiting loading on the F/A-18Cs of VFA-113 'Stingers', a Lemoore-based unit.

Below: Blue paint indicates a training store, here used for flight training for LGB designation.

used by the Argentines for extreme low-level attacks on British ships. Marine Corps F/A-18s used "snakes" for low level attacks on Iraqi troops in Kuwait during the Gulf War. 'Desert Storm' also saw the revival of a favorite weapons combination from the Vietnam era. "Snake and nape" — retarded bombs and napalm canisters — were delivered against Iraqi bunkers by Marine F/A-18s after the suppression of air defenses made low-angle attack passes relatively safe.

Bomblets are one of the F/A-18's main low-level weapons. If the weather turned bad, with low cloud preventing LGB delivery from medium altitude. Nickel Flight would probably be sent on its mission with bomblets, briefed to attack under the weather, staying below the effective envelope of most SAMs, and make level (or pitch-up) deliveries of the bomblets. Modern submunition weapons can deliver bomblets from as low as 400 feet or as high as 40,000 feet.

Bomblets can be delivered from submunition weapons such as the Mk 20 Rockeye cluster bomber unit (CBU). These are designed primarily for use against vehicles but also work against small naval targets. The Mk 20 is the same weight as a 500-lb bomb, but is filled with 247 Mk 118 bomblets.

The CBU-78 Gator is of a similar weight, but is instead filled with 45 antitank and 15 antipersonnel mines. Both types were extensively used in the Gulf War. Canadian CF-18s can use the British BL 755 bomblet weapon.

The F/A-18 can also carry weapons for the

(HOTAS) control at that instant. The use of laser technology means that F/A-18s are more accurate than F-16s. During the Gulf War, F/A-18s mainly used 1,000-pound Mk 83s, the iron bomb versions of the GBU-16s that Nickel Flight is delivering. This remains a standard weapon, along with the 500-lb. Mk 82 , and the heavy 2,000-lb. Mk 84.

All of these, (but most frequently the Mk 82), can be retarded. This allows them to be dropped from low altitude, retarding their drop while the attacking aircraft exits the fragmentation envelope. The standard US bomb retardation systems are the BDU-54 "balute" (a combination balloon and parachute) and the Mk 15 "Snakeye" (four metal retarding tail blades which open on dropping). "Snake" bombs became well-known in the Falklands War of 1982, when

suppression of enemy air defenses. These include AGM-88 HARMs, anti-radiation missiles (ARMs), which can home in on enemy radars, forcing them to be either turned off or destroyed. It can also carry ADM-141 Tactical Air Launch Decoys (TALD), gliding decoys which appear as an aircraft to enemy radar.

In addition to these weapons, a range of other precision guided munitions have become increasingly important, as demonstrated in the Gulf War of 1991. These include the long-range AGM-84E SLAM (Standoff Land Attack Missile).

As it is a naval aircraft, sinking ships is an important mission for the F/A-18. The Harpoon air-to-surface missile is the ideal weapon for this task, as it can be fired from over-the-horizon at the target ship. When Harpoon is not available, LGBs will be used against naval targets, as today. This was done against Libyan ships in 1986 and Iranian ships in 1988. In those actions, the LGBs were delivered by A-6Es.

Because the gunboats are sheltering among fishing boats, the target will have to be attacked visually. For that reason the F/A-18's main battery on this mission is a pair of GBU-16B Paveway II 1,000-pound laser-guided bombs.

F/A-18s can be used to deliver the full range of US Navy mines, though they have never done so. For the ultimate anti-ship capability, even though the US Navy no longer carries nuclear weapons on its carriers in peacetime, the F/A-18 is cleared to deliver the B61 tactical nuclear weapon.

Unguided weapons are also used against naval targets. In the Gulf War, Canadian CF-18s used 70-mm CVR-7 unguided rockets against Iraqi small craft, a weapon not carried by their US counterparts. The five-inch Zuni unguided rocket is carried by US F/A-18s as a target marker.

One of the most important missiles to this strike will not be launched by F/A-18s. Ships of the Carrier Battle Group will fire Tomahawk Land Attack Missiles (TLAMs) timed to hit the target just before the strike package comes into range.

TLAMs will not be fired against targets that may move while it is in the air, cruising in from the ships. It will rather be targeted against fixed or semi-fixed sites such as air defense or surface surveillance radars, fire control radars for the Silkworms, or command posts.

F/A-18 ARMAMENT

The Hornet can carry external loads up to a total of 17,000 lb (7,700 kg) on five principal stations, supplemented by the wingtip rails and two intake stations, which are normally used for sensors. Typical loads include four Mavericks or HARMs, or up to 10 general purpose or cluster bombs.

Right: The free-fall Mk83 LDGP bomb weighs 985 lb (447 kg), and is still used in large numbers, although it is not suited to low level release.

Below: The McDonnell Douglas AGM-84E SLAM (Standoff Land Attack Missile) is a derivative of the anti-ship Harpoon, with an imaging infrared seeker and GPS updating of the inertial navigation system.

Below: The Texas Instruments GBU-24 Paveway III laser-guided bomb is based on the 2,000 lb (900 kg) Mk84 bomb or BLU-109 penetration warhead. It weighs up to 2,350 lb (1,066kg).

Below: The CBU-87B/B CEM (Combined Effects Munition) is one form of the Mk7 cluster bomb dispenser. It releases 202 bomblets.

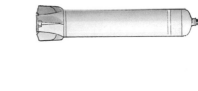

Right: Shown with its metal fins extended for maximum drag, the Mk82 Snakeye is widely used. Retarding the bomb enhances aircraft safety in low level delivery.

Below: The free-fall Mk82 LDGP bomb weighs 531 lb (240 kg), compared to the 570 lb (259 kg) of the Snakeye version.

Right: The GBU-12B/C/D Paveway II is the laser-guided version of the Mk82 bomb, and weighs 611 lb (277 kg). This series is distinguished from the Paveway I by its pop-out fins, making carriage easier.

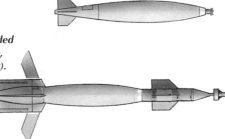

THE MISSION:
NICKEL FLIGHT

"**Man Your Planes.**" **The traditional US Navy command is passed to the aircrew in their squadron ready rooms. This is what the US government has been paying them for all these years. The F/A-18, now Nickel 01, has been brought up to the flight deck by the plane handlers on one of the four large hydraulic elevators positioned around the outboard edges of the flight deck. The F/A-18 has been "spotted", wings folded, in a flight-deck parking spot in accordance with a plan worked out by the carrier's Aircraft Handling Officer. He has to make sure that the aircraft the operational plan calls to be launched first does not become blocked from reaching the catapult.**

PRE-FLIGHT

Above: Checks are carried out on an F/A-18C of VFA-86 'Sidewinders'. Note the rattlesnake and top-hat insignia.

Nickel 01's pilot's first task is the same as that of any other pilot: conduct a thorough pre-flight inspection. Accompanied by the brown-jersey plane captain, the pre-flight is carried out first externally, then in the cockpit. They will look for dripping fluids, unsecured panels, foreign object debris (FOD), foreign objects or damage in the engine intakes, check fluid reservoirs and pressures, examine the engine exhausts, manually move control surfaces, and check lights.

The external walk-around inspection will look at the safety and fusing wires on the bombs, check the coolant for the AIM-9M Sidewinder missiles riding expectantly on the wingtip launch rails and check the radome on the longer-ranged AIM-120 AMRAAM.

The pilot and plane captain climb a platform ladder to perform the cockpit checks. Circuit breakers, ejection seat, and electrical system are among the most important stops on the check list. At the same time, Nickel 02's pilot and back-seater and their plane captain will be doing the same thing for their two-seat F/A-18D.

Checks completed — about a 45-minute process — Nickel 01's pilot signs the acceptance form, tightens his harnesses, and zips up his survival vest. After making a last inspection, he arms the SJU-5/6 ejection seat, pulling and stowing the red-tagged arming pins. Only then does he strap in. He then attaches the leg restraints to the flight suits, the fittings to the torso and shoulder harnesses, G-suit, oxygen mask, and helmet all have to be connected to the airplane. The F/A-18 and its pilot are now literally linked together as one entity, Nickel 01, for the duration of the mission. "For we are one, my sword and I ..."

START UP

The pilot now does the pre-start check list, shutting down any of the systems that could be damaged by a power surge as the engines are started. With the plane captain, having finished his checks, standing by, the pilot gives the "ready for power" signal.

The F/A-18 is now ready to start the engine, either by using a "huffer cart", a mobile external power source, or by using its own internal battery. The battery provides enough power to start the auxiliary power unit (APU) which in turn starts the engines — first the right, then the left — and runs the intercom between the pilot and the plane captain on the deck.

The pilot now checks the radios (and intercom) and uses built-in test equipment (BITE) to make sure that the wide range of systems on the F/A-18 actually work. He makes sure that all the required electrical systems are on-line and showing green.

After running up the engines, before clearance is given for taxiing, the pilot aligns the F/A-18's inertial navigation system (INS) in carrier-based "CV" mode. This is transmitted from the ship's INS (SINS). The INS has been pre-loaded with waypoints along the course to the target.

The deck is now loud with starting and running up engines. Even at this stage, the potential for disaster and heavy losses is very real. Fire-fighting crews in silver protective suits stand ready off the edge of the flight deck. White-shirted safety members of the deck crew watch for dangerous situations. The carrier's air department head, the "Air Boss" runs the show from the Primary Flight Operations Center, "Pri-Fly". The pilot then waits for direction from the "Air Boss" (who controls the hectic activity on the flight deck) to taxi to the catapult.

Above: Steam leaks from the catapult as the F/A-18C is readied for launch.

Below: The 'yellow jackets' align the Hornet with the catapult, while an EA-6B Prowler taxies forward to take its place in the launch sequence.

TAXI TO THE CAT

Nickel 01 receives the signal to taxi. A yellow-shirted plane director, standing in front of Nickel 01, motions it forward out of its deck-edge spot. The F/A-18 is now taking part in a potentially deadly bit of performance art choreographed from the carrier's island. The object is to move aircraft off the deck and into the air as quickly as possible but with complete safety.

The low residual thrust of the F/A-18's F404 engines requires a touch of throttle to get and keep it rolling on deck. The yellow shirts keep the pilot taxiing to the catapult, sometimes with the wheels up to the edge of the flight deck, and make sure the jet exhaust stays clear of other aircraft and personnel.

The F/A-18 will wait behind the retractable deflectors to protect it from the jet blast of the preceding aircraft. While waiting for the catapult, the pilot will do the takeoff checklist. While previous generations of fighter pilots had this on a kneeboard, the F/A-18's pilot pushes a button to call it up on the checklist display on the left Data Display

PREPARE TO LAUNCH

Nickel 01 is now next for the catapult. The steel wall of the jet blast deflector that protected it from the engines of the previous F/A-18, now climbing away from the ship, is lowered. Steam envelopes the waiting Nickel 01 as the catapult starts to build up pressure for the next shot.

Before taxiing into position, a green-shirted aircraftsman will hold up a board showing the weight of the F/A-18. The pilot will verify the F/A-18's gross weight — 40,700 pounds in the case of Nickel 01 — to appropriately set the catapult's thrust. Ordnancemen, wearing

Left: The catapult looks extremely short, but the acceleration it produces is eye-watering, and its task may be eased by a wind-over-deck speed of around 30 knots (55 km/hr).

CAT SHOT

The pilot again checks the flight controls, moving the stick and rudder pedals. The flaps and leading edge are set in proper position for maximum lift. Both rudders turn in to provide extra nose-up trim.

When the pilot receives the "final turnup" signal from the catapult officer standing by the edge of the flight deck — left arm forward, right arm back as if to hurl a javelin — he advances the throttles to MIL - maximum military (non-afterburner) power. While the F/A-18 can take off on full military power alone, Nickel 01 will use afterburner to take-off. The pilot advances the throttles to MAX and waits for the signal from the catapult officer, then cuts in the burners.

The pilot does one final check of the instruments, holds the throttles firmly against the detent, places his head back against the headrest, and salutes the catapult officer with his right hand. The catapult officer kneels down on the flight deck, checks forward and aft, and touches the deck. This is the signal to the catapult operator, just off the flight deck, to hit the launch button, unleashing the in-tension energy of the catapult.

Powered by steam from the ship's main engines, the catapult accelerates the F/A-18 from a dead stop to 125 knots in less than two seconds. The shock of the launch slams the pilot's helmet hard back against the headrest, but his hands remain on the throttle and stick.

Right: The jet blast deflector is raised behind the Hornet to protect following aircraft from the efflux of the aircraft's two General Electric F404 afterburning turbofans. This is evidently the personal aircraft of the officer commanding CVW-1.

Indicator (DDI) of the instrument panel. The pilot checks the flight controls. A few quick flicks of the wrist on the stick move the controls to their limits, a touch on the pedals does the same for the rudders.

The catapult launch is a complex procedure that has to be carried out quickly. The strike can be launched at a rate quicker than one aircraft every 30 seconds, with first three, then all four catapults working as the deck becomes less crowded. The first planes off the deck will be tankers (KA-6Ds and S-3s and F/A-18 with "buddy tank" pods under their wings), E-2Cs, S-3s, ES-3s and an F-14 CAP (to make sure no enemy tries to interfere with the battle group during the launch).

The Air Boss' representative on the flight deck, the flight-deck chief, prioritizes and directs aircraft moving toward the catapults. This is important because the catapult must be reset after each launch if the aircraft are of different weights and types, increasing the time required to launch the strike.

red jerseys, pull red-flagged restraining pins and check fusing wires to arm the F/A-18's underslung weapons load. A last-chance checker, wearing a checked jersey, does a final external inspection of the F/A-18.

The plane director will direct the pilot to slowly taxi into the catapult track. The F/A-18 taxis past the catapult shuttle to hook its nosewheel launch bar up to the catapult. The green-shirted catapult crew will install the holdback bar to the linkage, designed to keep the airplane steady until the catapult builds up to the required level of force for launch.

Right: At last, the Hornet pilot receives the 'final turnup' signal from the catapult officer and pushes the throttles forward to provide maximum non afterburning thrust.

CLIMBING TO ALTITUDE

Immediately, the pilot raises the landing gear and makes the mandatory radio call. "Nickel 01, airborne."
As soon as the F/A-18 reaches minimum flap retraction speed the pilot starts to slowly retract the big, high-lift flaps, but not too fast, as they will provide more lift than drag until the F/A-18's speed comes up.

As the F/A-18 starts to climb — at a 30 degree angle until speed comes up to 250 knots — he leaves the carrier's departure radio frequency. He had been talking to the Carrier Air Traffic Control Center. This is the carrier's air traffic control system, and its controllers bring the aircraft onto and away from the carrier.

The pilot now switches to another radio pre-set — each of the two basic UHF radios have up to 20 pre-set channels — with the strike frequency. Talking with "Strike" connects him with the carrier's Combat Direction Center, the nerve center of the battle group.

It is possible for the F/A-18 to dispense with many of these radio calls. Since realizing how electronically noisy its operations were in the 1970s, the US Navy has been practicing operations at different levels of EMCOM (emissions control). A strike could be run with no voice communications from launch to recovery if required.

The fly-out from the carrier is at low altitude, 500-1,000 feet, until five to seven miles distant. The F/A-18 also checks its two IFF systems, Mode 1-3 "Parrot" and secure Mode 4 "India". Other systems that are mission critical are also checked.

Later, Nickel Flight will be netted in with Hummer 01, an E-2C radar aircraft serving as a strike controller. Hummer 01 will confirm he has Nickel 01's "skin paint" — the radar return from the airframe — on his radar, plus his "Parrot" and "India" (code for the IFF transponder). Nickel Flight carriers carries out a "running rendezvous", with both F/A-18s responding to vectors from the E-2C to join up en route to the target. Nickel Flight — Nickel O2 is now joining up — will rely on secure UHF voice communications — with the beep and shush of the KY-58 encrypting device punctuating messages — for most of the flight.

Left: Hornet 401 is set to go, while its stablemate 403 is catapulted from the angled deck, condensation streaming from its wingtips as the vortices cool the humid air.

IN THE COCKPIT

When it was introduced, in the early 1980s, the F/A-18 cockpit was the most advanced in the world and represented a significant advance over such fighters as the F-15. The buzzword for modern combat aircraft is increasing the pilot's "situational awareness". That is why it appears different from the ranks of dials and indicators that used to characterize a previous generation of combat aircraft.

While the appearance of the F/A-18's cockpit is new, it reflects truths about air combat known since the Great War. In combat, a pilot's head is spinning around like a top. The last thing a pilot wants to do is to have to look inside the cockpit, at an instrument. Similarly, the pilot's hands will be firmly attached to the controls and throttle. Having to reach or grope for another control

is definitely something to be avoided. By the time the F/A-18 was in production, technology had provided at least a partial answer to these two problems. One is the Head-Up Display (HUD), the other is Hands On Throttle and Stick (HOTAS) controls.

Together, all of these elements provide not only technological innovation, but superior capability. The F/A-18's cockpit is 40% smaller than that of one of the naval aircraft it replaced, the A-7. The F/A-18 requires only 350 square inches of instrument panel. The two cockpits of the F-4 — the other naval aircraft replaced by the F/A-18 — required no less than 2,700 square inches.

This saving in space meant less of a volume had to be devoted to the cockpit, more to avionics and fuel.

Below: This wide-angle portrait of Major M G Rolling of VMFA(AW)-224 demonstrates the exceptional all-round visibility of the Hornet, the vertical tail being clearly seen.

THE COCKPIT

THE HEAD UP DISPLAY

The information the pilot absolutely has to know to stay alive in combat — and defeat his or her opponents — is brought up to eye level by the Head Up Display (HUD).

The HUD puts speed, heading, weapons status, aiming cues, altitude, warning lights all before the pilot's eyes. Just as the HOTAS means that the F/A-18 pilot's hands can stay in one place during combat, his eyes never have to go inside the cockpit. The pilot will be looking through the HUD or at the airspace around him. The data from the small three-inch bearing display of the ALR-67 radar homing and warning (RHAW) system will display the bearing of threats to the F/A-18 and their strength can also be projected onto the HUD.

If an F/A-18 is carrying an AAR-50 TINS pod, the HUD will also display the thermal landscape and the objects in it on the HUD. In this way, even at night, the pilot looking through the HUD can "see" reference points. FLIR data from the underslung AAS-38B Nite Hawk pod can also be projected onto the HUD.

The HUD is important not only in combat, but in navigation. Data such as distance and bearing to beacons, position, and other information can be selected to be displayed on the HUD. The F/A-18's HUD is designed for carrier landings, and will display the "needles" of the Instrument Landing System (ILS) that the pilot uses to stay on the glide slope.

RADAR DISPLAYS

In both air-air and air-ground modes, the APG-73 radar can be used to both search for targets and then lock onto and track them for attack. In the air-to-air mode, missiles such as the AIM-120 AMRAAM can be fired against aircraft beyond visual range, detected only on radar. Other information is displayed in the cockpit on a range of digital instruments. In typical fighter cockpit style, these are spread on both sides of the cockpit as well as below and to the sides of the DDIs.

THE MULTIPURPOSE DISPLAY GROUP

The multipurpose display group is the heart of the instrument panel. In addition to the HUD, it consists of the two large cathode ray tubes (CRTs). Surrounded by selector buttons are the Data Display Indicators (DDIs). The Horizontal Indicator (HI), the heading switch, and the course set switch make up the rest of these key instruments.

The pilot can view a wide range of checklists and flight and status instruments by simply hitting the right button around the perimeter of the DDIs. For example, the left display on the cockpit can, at the touch of a button, either display the detailed weapons status of all the ordnance carried on board the F/A-18 or show television-like infrared images from the FLIR. With a flick of a function switch, the pilot can call up on the digital display any of the information about the aircraft that its computerized internal sensors tell. Should a warning light on the annunciator panel light, the pilot could call up engine temperature, status, fuel state, and a number of indicators that would, in a previous generation of aircraft, each have had to be shown by a specific analog instrument or gauge on a panel. In fact, knowing which function switches to push and being able to select them successfully under all conditions are key skills that must be acquired when a pilot transitions to F/A-18s.

Below the two monochrome DDIs is the Horizontal Indicator (HI), a third, similar but full-color screen that will primarily act as a moving map display, providing aircraft attitude, steering, and navigation information. The center HI is the full-color moving map display for the APG-73 multi-mode radar. At the push of a button, the radar can either go into navigation mode, air-to-air mode (looking ahead, up and down for targets) or air-to-ground mode (in which it looks down, producing a radar map). In air-air or air-ground mode, its returns will usually be displayed in the right DDI.

At the top of the instrument panel, under the HUD, is the Upfront Control. This multifunction control panel selects autopilot modes, controls the IFF system, the instrument landing system (ILS), handles navigation through the TACAN and ADF. It also controls the UHF radios and datalink.

HANDS ON THROTTLE AND STICK (HOTAS)

STICK

1 Nosewheel steering and autopilot disengage
2 Nosewheel steering off button
3 Weapon select
4 Trigger
5 Air/ground weapon release
6 Sensor control
7 Pitch and roll trim switch
8 Pitch and roll control handle

THROTTLE

1 Speed brake control
2 Cage/uncage button
3 Communications selector
4 Flare/chaff switch
5 Radar antenna elevation control
6 Exterior lights
7 RAID/FLIR select button
8 ATC engage/disengage (automatic throttle)
9 Designator controller
10 Throttle control slides (forward to increase, back to decrease)

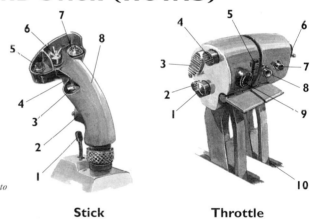

Stick   **Throttle**

Just as the most important information is brought before the pilot's eyes by the HUD, the most important actions can be performed by simply moving a finger. The F/A-18's Hands On Throttle and Stick (HOTAS) concept means that in combat the pilot will be able to grasp these two controls and not have to reach around the cockpit. This is more than simple ergonomics, it may be a matter of life and death. At the high G-forces encountered in modern fighter combat, even moving an arm in the cockpit could prove difficult as well as distracting.

The HOTAS concept has resulted in the barnacle-encrusted appearance of the F/A-18's throttle and the stick. Each of the buttons and switches has a different, but vital, function. By holding onto the throttle and stick, a flick of the finger can, once they are armed, fire any of the F/A-18's weapons or activate any of the aircraft's sensors.

The F/A-18, unlike the F-16, has its stick in the traditional position, between the pilot's knees. It includes one element that would be instantaneously recognizable to an earlier generation of fighter pilots: the pistol trigger. Other additions to the stick include the electric trim button, the nosewheel steering, autopilot control, radar mode and air-air weapons selectors and a separate weapons release button for air-surface weapons.

The stick activates digital fly-by-wire flight controls, with purely mechanical control of the all-flying "tailerons" possible as a back-up. The control system will automatically return the aircraft to level flight if the pilot releases the controls: a useful capability if approaching a loss of control situation.

The two throttles — the F/A-18 is a twin-engine aircraft — have between them the communications transmit switch, the chaff and flare dispenser selector and trigger button, the speed brake selector switch, the autothrottle engage and disengage switch (for automatic controlled carrier landings) and several radar selection switches. Two finger rests allow the pilot to accomplish most of these tasks with a flick of the finger tip.

REFUELING EN ROUTE

Left: A Hornet with probe extended refuels from a USAF KC-135. Designed to refuel USAF aircraft via 'receptacles', the Boeing 'flying boom' is fitted here with a hose and drogue to suit USN/USMC aircraft.

Right: The KC-135R refuels an F-14 from VFA-101 'Grim Reapers', based at NAS Oceana, while a bombed-up F/A-18D from VMFA(AW)-224 waits its turn.

Because Nickel flight's target, an Iranian gunboat, is separated from the other targets of the strike — Silkworm missile launchers, their command centers, and the SAM sites defending them — the two F/A-18s are flying largely by themselves in a "combat spread" two-ship formation, abeam and about a mile apart.

Nickel Flight has to hit a tanker to refuel on its way to the target. Unless refueled, the F/A-18's radius of action with a full weapons load is limited. A fully loaded F/A-18 may be able to fly for as little as 30-40 minutes without refueling. Nickel 01 took off with about 13,000 pounds of JP5 fuel in its 1,600-gallon internal tanks and its 330-gallon belly tank. Nickel 01, once it climbs to cruise altitude, will get about .085 nautical miles per pound of fuel burned.

The first step is to find the tanker. Nickel Flight has been briefed as to the expected location of the refueling track and the time they are planned to tank. With most of the air wing's F/A-18s committed to the mission and very thirsty, there will be a shortage of tankers and a need for precise planning. Later, as the

strike recovers, other tankers will be waiting on the way home. At least one tanker will be waiting overhead as the strike recovers, for aircraft that miss their approach and run short of fuel.

The F/A-18s can use their radars in air-to-air search mode to locate the tanker. The tanker also has a VHF navigation beacon for homing. At night, it can flash a powerful strobe light. In peacetime, VHF radio from the tanker, E-2C or "strike" back on the carrier can be used to vector the flight to the tanker. This being an operational mission, the refueling will be accomplished with as little transmission as possible.

Nickel Flight is to be refueled by Texaco 01, a Navy tanker launched from the carrier before the rest of the strike. A-6Es with "buddy tanker" stores or KA-6D tankers are leaving service in the late 1990s as the Air Force takes over more of the Navy's tanking duties. F/A-18s are also used as "buddy tankers", as can S-3s when required. But F/A-18s cannot match the KA-6D's capacity of four 200-gallon internal fuel cells and an equal number of 330-gallon external tanks.

Nickel Flight comes up astern of the tanker. While refueling can be accomplished under total radio silence conditions, UHF voice radio will be used to coordinate with the tanker.

"Nickel 01, astern, nose cold, all switches safe, looking for 5.0."

The F/A-18 pilot specifies how many thousand pounds of fuel Nickel 01 is scheduled to receive. If the tanker is short on fuel, he may ask "Texaco 01, say give": how many thousand pounds of fuel he has available.

Once Nickel 01 has been cleared by Texaco 01 to commence an approach, the pilot checks his radar is off, double-checks his weapons switches are safe, extends the F/A-18's retractable air refuel probe, and calls up the air refueling check list on left cockpit DDI.

As Nickel 01 approaches, the tanker is streaming its drogue, stabilizing below its slipstream some 10-15 feet behind the tanker. The F/A-18 pilot trims the airplane for a stabilized approach, watches for the amber "ready" light on the tanker, and then slightly increases power to create a closure rate with

the tanker of two to five knots, pushing the probe into the drogue's basket. Nickel 01 must now push the drogue and hose forward a few feet to start the fuel flow, which will be evident as the tanker's amber light turns to green.

As the fuel flows — a thousand pounds a minute is standard flow rate from a tanker, less from a buddy-tank — Nickel 01 flies a close tail-chase formation with the tanker. This need not be a straight line, and the F/A-18's pilot may have to keep the fuel flow going even as the tanker changes altitude or turns. While Nickel 01 is preoccupied, his wingman keeps a lookout for potential problems and waits his turn.

When the F/A-18 has received its scheduled fuel, it goes through the engagement procedure in reverse and disengages its refueling probe, reducing power to achieve a three to five knot separation rate. The probe will disengage when the hose reaches full extension. Nickel 01 can now retract the probe and pull back as Nickel 02 approaches for his refueling. The whole procedure has lasted about eight minutes. Nickel 01 will now fly Nickel 02's wing as he refuels.

NAVIGATING

Below: Here two F/A-18Cs from the USS America form up behind the tanker. Note the carriage of AIM-7 Sparrow medium-range air-to-air missiles on the intake duct stations.

Finding small targets in the midst of large areas of ocean is what naval aircraft are designed to do and their crews are trained to be good at it. Nickel Flight has a good idea of where the gunboat is operating. To get there, it will use the F/A-18's ASN-130A inertial navigation system (INS) (which can be updated in flight from data from TACAN beacons or GPS). This is the primary system because it is autonomous and, once run up from the ship's system before launch, keeps the F/A-18 on course without reliance on any outside beacons. The F/A-18's advanced system is highly accurate and its position-keeping slips as little as 1.5 nautical miles per hour.

The F/A-18s fly to the pre-programmed series of waypoints in their INSs. En route steering cues with "Fly to" markers appear on the HUD. The HI in the cockpit displays navigation symbols and digital readouts from all the F/A-18s navigation systems. These include direction, distance and time-to-go to the next INS waypoint. This is all superimposed on the multicolor moving map display with an aircraft symbol superimposed over an aeronautical chart showing the F/A-18's current position and heading.

Global Position System (GPS) capability has been retrofitted to many F/A-18s. Using the differential timing of reception of radio signals from the constellation of GPS radio satellites, GPS is so accurate that an F/A-18 could attack an area target simply by bombing on the coordinates.

The ARN-118 Tactical Air Navigation (TACAN) system is a VHF radio beacon. Warships and aircraft such as tankers have a

TACAN beacon, which allows the F/A-18 to home in on their position. The Distance Measurement Equipment (DME) determines the range to the TACAN beacon.

One of the Aegis cruisers of the battle group has been forward deployed, close to the target. If required, this cruiser can back up the E-2Cs as a strike controller. It can also, if required, turn on its TACAN beacon to provide an offset marker for the incoming strike, as was done with F/A-18s attacking Libya in 1986. What makes Nickel Flight appreciate the cruiser most as they pass overhead is the forward-deployed HH-60H combat search and rescue helicopter ready on its fantail.

The APG-73 radar has a navigation mode. This shows a ground map of the terrain the F/A-18 is flying over. At sea, it can detect ships and islands at long range. It currently lacks the full synthetic aperture radar (SAR) mapping capability of the F-15E's similar APG-70 radar, though this will be provided to F/A-18Ds under the Phase II planned Radar Upgrade (RUG) program. Then, the APG-73 will be able to provide either high-resolution mapping of a ten nautical mile strip with point-target spotlight mode for identifying specific targets. But even today the APG-73 gives the pilot the capability to select a detailed map display when in navigation mode.

The inputs from all of these navigation systems are integrated in the F/A-18's Mission Computer 1 (MC1) which displays the results on the navigation screen on the center HI on the instrument panel. Its moving map display shows the location of the F/A-18 over standard aeronautical charts, digitized and stored on a CD-ROM.

IDENTIFICATION FRIEND OR FOE (IFF)

Throughout the strike, Nickel Flight will be carrying out IFF procedures. One of the trickiest parts of any air combat operation is identifying who is on which side. Before takeoff, the appropriate IFF code was entered to permit the carrier and E-2Cs to "interrogate" the F/A-18 and verify that it is on our side. Because the enemy has an ability to use IFF transponders to detect friendly aircraft, in many tactical situations the non-secure transponder will be turned off ("strangling the parrot").

No IFF system is foolproof. The strike controllers will keep track of all friendly aircraft and make sure that they are where they are supposed to be. As the strike returns to the carrier, the forward deployed Aegis cruiser will "delouse" the returning strike, identifying which are returning friendly aircraft, possibly with damaged IFFs, and which are enemy aircraft trying to repeat the old Japanese Second World War tactic of following a returning strike back to the carrier.

Above: The rear cockpit of the F/A-18D lacks the pilot's head-up display, but it has the three multi-function displays. The center one is showing a ground map generated by the APG-73 radar.

OPENING THE SHOW:

Jamming

The strike, including Nickel flight, is now approaching the target. Cruising at high or medium altitude — most aircraft have climbed to over 30,000 feet to reduce fuel consumption — it will not have the element of surprise. To stay under the Iranian radar coverage would have limited the range and payload of the strike. However, the strike can surprise the Iranians as to how many aircraft there are and where they are headed.

Here, as throughout the mission, Nickel 01 can count on a broad range of support. The two EA-6Bs will commence stand-off jamming, flying race-track patterns some 60 nautical miles away from the enemy radars and using their five powerful ALQ-99 jammers for barrage jamming of enemy radars, starting with the long-range early warning radars.

In the Gulf War, EA-6Bs were designated a mission-critical asset. That meant that if they could not support a mission, the Navy would turn around all the F/A-18s. EA-6B operators say they can shut down most of the US east coast with two airplanes, so they seldom get to radiate full power in peacetime. On this mission, the Iranian early warning and fire control radars are a mix of US-, British-, Russian- and Chinese-built systems. Thus, the barrage jammers will have to cover a broad range of frequencies.

To make sure this jamming power is being applied to the right radars, the EA-6Bs each have a computerized ESM system. It detects the frequency of each enemy radar it intercepts. The system's central processing unit then tasks one or more of the five jamming pods to radiate power in the correct direction and at the correct frequency.

As a result of this noise jamming, where the enemy radar was intending to receive back the electronic echo of its signal bouncing off a target, it receives instead a massive "noise" that blankets out the return rather than a single return. All the radar operator sees along the bearing that the EA-6B is jamming is solid white on the radar screen.

Above: This pair of F/A-18Ds from VMFA(AW)-224 illustrate some of the Hornet's many armament options. The 'BM' tail-code suggests the aircraft is operating with VMFA-451, co-based at Beaufort.

Decoy Attacks

Even the most powerful jamming has a "burn through" range, at which the power of the enemy signal is so strong the radar will see the returning echo despite the jamming. The answer to this is to provide the enemy with many more spurious targets than real ones. The strike will do this by launching ADM-141 Tactical Air Launched Decoys (TALD).

The TALD is designed to appear like a fighter on enemy radar. Launched from F/A-18s at high altitude — from 40,000 feet it has a range of 70 nautical miles — the TALD is a glider with folding wings that is carried on underwing pylons in place of bombs. It can also be fitted to drop chaff or burn an infrared flare to simulate a jet exhaust. The TALD was used extensively by F/A-18s during the Gulf War.

By firing TALDs, the strike is going to make the Iranian defenders' lives much more interesting. The TALDs will serve as a diversion and as exciters. Iranian attention and radar energy alike will be focused on them rather than the actual aircraft. Iranian fire control radars will 'light up' and start to track the TALDs, making the fire control radars vulnerable to attack by AGM-88 anti-radiation missiles (HARMs). Some TALDs will go on to be engaged by Iranian SAMs, draining away part of the defense.

Cruise Missile attack

Just as the game is starting to get interesting for the Iranian air defense radars — having to deal with both jamming and decoys — it suddenly comes to a painful and humiliating end for many of them.

Within two minutes, as the strike is approaching the targets, all the static Iranian air defense radars, SAM and AAA fire control radars, the Silkworm sites, and a nearby forward airfield, are hit by a coordinated time-on-target strike by Tomahawk Land Attack Missiles (TLAMs). The TLAMs were launched by the forward-deployed cruiser, destroyer and submarines of the carrier battle group. Because of the TLAM's long flight times and the fact that they would have to be targeted in advance of the strike, they are being used against static or semi-static targets that were not likely to move in the time between strike planning and missiles arriving on the target. Depending on the target characteristics, the TLAMs will carry either a unitary high explosive warhead or will eject submunitions to cover a larger area.

The TLAM's ability to use terrain comparison "TERCOM" guidance in flight at low altitude over land was used to permit diversionary routing, increasing the element of surprise. The TLAMs crossed the coast outside the radar range of the main Iranian defenses. Once inland, the TLAMs flew parallel to the coast until arriving behind their targets. The TLAMs then turned and struck them from the landward side — where the air defenses have not been set up to defend against an attack. Even if some of the incoming TLAMs are spotted, they will add to the confusion of the decoy attacks.

The use of TLAMs in coordination with the carrier strike is one of the ways both can be used synergistically, rather than having one substitute for another. The TLAMs increase the effect of the carrier strike by hitting enemy radars and air defenses as the aircraft are coming into range. Even if the radars are not knocked out by the TLAMs themselves, they are likely to be disrupted for long enough to avoid losses to the carrier strike. The strike will be able to assess the damage caused by the TLAMs. The TLAM attack will be timed to begin soon enough for some of the smoke of impact to have dissipated, but not long enough to allow the Iranians to recover from the attack.

Left: The beauty of an MFD is that it can display flight instruments, navigation data, weapon status, checklists, a radar map, or (as here) a TV or FLIR image of the terrain or the target.

The SLAMs Arrive

Following the TLAM strike are several AGM-84E Stand-off Land Attack Missiles (SLAMs) fired from modified F/A-18s some 60 nautical miles away from the target. Because of its long range (reportedly up to 120 nautical miles), high cost and high capability, only a few F/A-18s are fitted for SLAM and currently only about a quarter of deployed F/A-18 pilots are trained in using it.

The SLAM is a modified version of the Harpoon anti-ship missile. It uses inertial guidance, updated with GPS, for the highly accurate terminal homing required by its mission as a bunker-buster, destroying hardened facilities such as those associated with the Silkworm missile batteries. For terminal homing, the SLAM has the same imaging infrared (IIR) seeker as an AGM-65D Maverick missile, which the GPS-updated INS keeps pointed at the target. The missile uses the AWW-13, an improved version of the video datalink used by the older Walleye PGM.

When the SLAM enters its terminal phase, about one minute before impact, the IIR seeker is activated and sends back a picture of what it is seeing to the guiding F/A-18 (which is not the same as the firing one). The picture will appear on a DDI on the F/A-18's instrument panel. The pilot then selects the precise aim point (such as the access door to a bunker) on the IIR image he wishes the SLAM to hit, putting cross hairs on the target's image. Once the aim point selection is transmitted back to the incoming SLAM, it becomes a fire and forget missile. It will home in exactly on the designated spot. The F/A-18 is then free to carry out other missions, such as joining the TARCAP against air threats.

LIGHTING UP

As soon as an enemy radar "lights up" (either an early warning radar which is used to detect and track the strike or a fire control radar, cued by the early warning radar as to the location of a US aircraft, trying to guide a surface to air missile or anti-aircraft artillery fire against it), the radar becomes a threat to the strike but is also vulnerable. It can reveal its location to a range of US aircraft. The strike is being supported by a wide range of passive sensors, which are those that do not radiate electronic power themselves, like a radar does, but passively receive the radiation of those that do radiate.

Above: The weapon system operator (WSO) is a vital member of the team in both air-to-air and air-to-ground operations. The yellow badge indicates this 'backseater' is a member of Marine Air Group No3.

Every airplane in the strike has a passive radar receiver. "Whale 01", the ES-3A that is orbiting a little further out from the E-2C, supporting the strike, has a highly capable ALR-76 ESM suite. It has a dedicated datalink connection back to the carrier so that the carrier's strike control will know what radars are switched on over the horizon.

The ES-3A will be among the first likely to pick up the radar. So will the EA-6Bs, with their sensitive ESM and multiple antennas and computerized threat libraries, which compare the signals it is receiving with those collected through electronic intelligence (ELINT) in the days and weeks preceding the conflict.

The first Iranian radars to be detected will be early warning radars. Most of these are mechanically swept arrays, so the ESM will only detect each radar every ten or more seconds as it sweeps around.

What is most dangerous to the F/A-18 is when the fire control radars light up. Once the fire control radar tracks the aircraft and develops a fire control solution, a surface to

air missile (SAM) can be fired and guided. Because fire control radars tend to have narrow directional beams rather than the broad sweep of a warning radar, they are much harder to detect.

Aircraft in or near the directional beam of a fire control radar may detect it. More significantly, because they may only track an aircraft for a few seconds before a missile is fired, fire control radars received on an aircraft's ESM is an indication of a very clear and present danger.

The F/A-18 is equipped with a smaller, self-defense ESM system. The ALR-67 radar homing and warning (RHAW) data has its own visual display in the cockpit. It provides the pilot with a visual cue as to the bearing, strength of signal, and displays the type of radar. This information is also repeated on the HUD. It can also provide an aural cue into the pilot's radio earphones. RHAW gear cannot perform the triangulation of position of more sophisticated ESM systems. But it does give the pilot a vital indication to start countermeasures to a missile.

The ALR-67 systems on Nickel Flight alert the pilots. Each display shows a code number associated with the type of fire control radar that is starting to track them.

The pilot of Nickel 01 looks at the bearing line shown for the fire control radar. He thinks it may be possibly from another ship escorting the Iranian gunboat that is his target or a shore-based SAM battery directly behind the gunboat, on the beach.

Even though there is no precise range information provided by the ALR-67, the CVIC briefing of the likely location of enemy SAMs and their associated fire control radars gives Nickel 01 a good idea of the likely range. Nickel 01 has a number of options to deal with the fire control radar. He can dive, trying to get below the coverage of the radar, using the curvature of the earth. The F/A-18s also have their own jammers and chaff. They can also maneuver to take maximum advantage of the EA-6B's stand-off jamming.

The option Nickel 01 decides on using is hanging under his F/A-18's wings: AGM-88 Highspeed Anti-Radiation Missiles (HARMs). Nickel 01 has already selected the HARM's station on his air-ground weapons selector switch before he turned on the master safety switch, arming all weapons. That his weapons are "hot" and that he has selected HARMs on the appropriate underwing pylons also appears on the HUD.

There will be two types of HARM shots fired as part of the strike. Most will be pre-planned HARM shots fired by "Iron Hand" F/A-18s. These are dedicated HARM shooters. Some will fire off their missiles on a precise schedule, covering a range of bearings and radar frequencies as the strike is nearing the target and then fly TARCAP to cover the withdrawal of the strike. Other Iron Hands will hold onto their HARMS and fire them off to cover the strike's withdrawal. These pre-planned shots make sure that for the few minutes while the strike is within the lethal envelope of enemy SAMs, any Iranian turning on a fire control radar does so at their peril.

The other type of HARM shots are like those Nickel 01 is about to take. F/A-18 "strikers" may carry one or two HARMs for self-defense. If they detect an enemy fire control radar, they will turn down the bearing line toward it and fire. Because the ALR-67 only shows the bearing and strength of signal, Nickel 01 selects "Bearing Only/Range Unknown" mode for the HARM launch.

Without the massive use of HARMs, the strike would have to be flown at low altitude, trying to stay underneath SAM coverage. While the US Navy practices these tactics, especially for smaller strikes where there is less potential for mutual support and in high intensity conflicts where it would be difficult to overcome the SAM threat, low-altitude tactics have the potential to put the attackers down within range of automatic anti-aircraft artillery or, more significantly, man-portable heat-seeking surface-to-air missiles.

Nickel 01 now turns to the bearing of the threat heading that the HUD shows the ALR-67 has detected the radar. From the Rules of Engagement determined at the briefing he does not have to clear such self-defense use of HARMs at this time, because there are no friendly radar emitters in the direction of the threat fire control radar. In the past, "blue on blue" friendly fire incidents have resulted from mistakes in using anti-radiation missiles, including a US Navy destroyer hit off Vietnam and a B-52 damaged during the Gulf War after a HARM fired from above homed in on its tail gun radar.

The pilot now pushes the air-surface button on the top of the stick and gives a warning call over the UHF radio.

"Nickel 01, Magnum."

The passive radar seeker in the nose of each HARM is already pointed along the bearing the enemy radar is radiating from. This gives it the bearing to fly if launched in "range unknown" mode. Inertial guidance and autopilot keep it on its high-speed Mach 2+ flight. If the enemy radar stays lit up and

working, the HARM will continue to home in on its location. If the enemy, aware of the incoming HARM, shuts down their radar, the HARM may still have a good enough solution for the HARM's laser proximity fuze to detonate its pre-fragmented warhead of thousands of tungsten cubes, able to perforate radar antennas over a wide area.

After the HARMs are launched, Nickel Flight makes a hard diving turn, hoping that enemy radar, even if not destroyed by the HARM attack, will have to shut down. Once it lights up again, the fire control radar would have to be re-cued by the early warning and target acquisition radars (now largely destroyed by the TLAMs), and would not find the F/A-18s in the narrow beams of their fire control radars. In any event, the HARM shot has caused the fire control radar to lose track and gives Nickel Flight more time to reach their target.

Above: These F/A-18Cs bear the 'AC' tail-code of CVW-3, which at time of writing is assigned to the USS Theodore Roosevelt. It consists of one Marine and two Navy Hornet squadrons, one squadron of F-14s, one of E-2Cs, one of SH-60s, one of EA-6Bs and one of S-3Bs.

WINGMAN

Keeps look-out for air threat or SAM launches while 'Nickel 01' is busy on its bomb run.

BOMB RELEASE

The bomb is released using the angle rate system. For maximum accuracy the aircraft flies at a steady speed, straight and level.

FINS

Delayed deployment wings stabilize the bomb's descent and impart a slow spin, giving a spiral scanning pattern to the laser light detector.

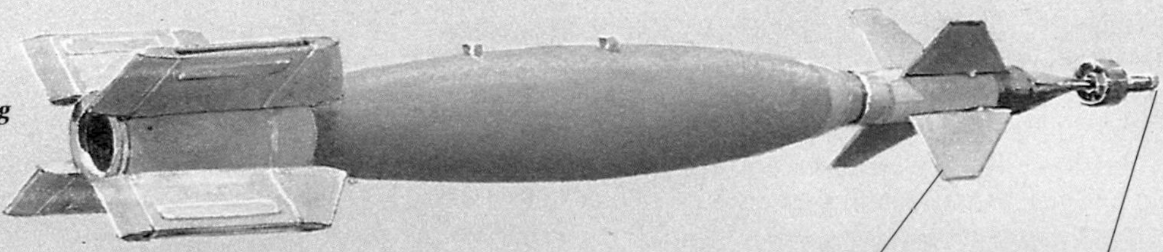

Guide vanes

Laser light detector

BOMBS AWAY

Nickel 01 now makes sure that his air-surface weapons selector switch is set to release the bombs and does the armament checklist (which can be called up on a DDI if required) for the attack. As always, the last step is to turn on the master arm switch, to avoid a premature release if the pilot inadvertently hits the air-surface release trigger on the top of the HOTAS stick.

Nickel 01 begins his approach to the target at 20,000 feet and 350-450 knots, keeping up an external scan for ground fire or a missile launch. "Speed is life" even when there is little apparent opposition, but as the F/A-18 will pick up speed quickly in a dive, the roll-in speed is kept down to prevent too fast a dive not giving the seeker heads on the bombs enough time to acquire the laser designation.

From the initial point (IP), programmed into the F/A-18's INS, Nickel 01 flies a base leg preparatory to his dive-bombing attack. The radar and FLIR both remain locked onto the gunboat as long as it remains within their field of view. Approaching the roll-in point, Nickel 01 calls in hot to the E-2C (indicating that he has armed his weapons and is about to attack).

The roll-in is a hard, diving turn to the attack heading. Nickel 01 "leads" the turn, as in the landing pattern, to make sure he rolls on the pre-briefed heading for the attack. This can be important for a number of factors, such as to make sure that the attack is coming out of the sun (in daylight) or to make sure that the attacking aircraft is coming from a direction where a stand-off jammer will help protect it against any radar-directed enemy air defense weapons.

Nickel 01's pilot pulls the nose up and rolls in, inverted. He sights the gunboat visually in the HUD. The F/A-18 rolls back upright, wings level, in a 45 degree dive. The seeker heads on the two GBU-16s will be looking to acquire the laser designation provided by Nickel 02, with a flight track about 30 degrees offset from Nickel 01's inbound heading. Nickel 01's speed quickly increases to about 450-550 knots.

The gunboat is not able to effectively resist the F/A-18's attacks. If a fire control radar is turned on, it will result in a HARM being fired at it. The F/A-18s are above the effective range of the gunboats' AAA and any heat-seeking SAMs it may be carrying.

The laser-guided bomb not only provides high accuracy, it reduces the F/A-18's exposure to defenses because it does not have to overfly the target and can remain at medium altitude with no loss of accuracy. An attacking F/A-18C can drop its bombs over three nautical miles away and sharply turn away if required.

DESIGNATOR

Target designation is carried out by a two-seat F/A-18. The infra-red and laser designator is mounted on the right of the fuselage. The aircraft flies a righthand orbit or race track to keep contact with the target.

FINDING AND IDENTIFYING THE TARGET

The gunboat has been located by increasingly more specific and accurate sensors. National intelligence means — satellites and airborne and shore-based ELINT — have provided information. The data is passed to the carrier through the TENCAP (Tactical Exploitation of National Capabilities) Program.

If shore-based naval assets were available, stand-off radar surveillance of the gunboat would have been carried out by shore-based P-3C Orions. EP-3E Orions would join the carrier-based ES-3As monitored enemy radar and communications use.

From the carrier, S-3B Vikings will carry out surface surveillance missions with their APQ-137 ISAR radars as well as looking for submarines. Hummer 01, the E-2C Hawkeye controlling the strike, will be looking for any air opposition as well as monitoring radar emissions. The E-2C's radar does not detect surface targets such as the gunboat. However, the E-2C's datalinks allow him to receive information from other platforms such as the ES-3A and an S-3B and to pass that information on to the F/A-18s over the voice radio. The F/A-18s will also ask the E-2C for a pilot weather report (PIREP) and threat report as they approach the target's position.

Above: The F/A-18Cs of VMFA-122 'Crusaders' bear a distinctive heraldic shield as their squadron badge. In this instance their weapon loads include Maverick and Sparrow missiles.

Radar Search

Once the radar has been taken out of navigation and put into air-ground mode, the gunboat can be acquired and then designated. As the F/A-18 comes closer to the gunboat, the radar coverage range automatically drops and increases the resolution of coverage. By the time the F/A-18s have the target on their APG-73 radars, there will be little doubt about where they are. The HUD and the moving map display on the HI shows the steering information to the offset target pre-entered into the F/A-18's INS. The F/A-18 can automatically cue its radar to search starting at the INS coordinates entered as the likely target location.

By the time the range has closed to 20 miles — outside the range of most of SAMs — the gunboat is clearly displayed on the radar scope display, although the range at which a naval target can be detected depends on its size and the sea state. Once the pilot puts a diamond designator symbol on the radar return from the gunboat on the display, the radar will automatically reduce the range scale as the F/A-18 gets closer. The radar will continue to search at increasingly finer resolution and then lock onto the target, displaying bomb release information to the pilot on the HUD and the on the radar display that can be called up on a DDI.

FLIR Search

Nickel Flight will confirm the target is the Iranian gunboat by using their AAS-38B FLIR systems. Using first a wide-area search mode slaved to the radar and then a fine resolution for target identification, the F/A-18 can thus "eyeball" a target on the darkest night (but not through low cloud, which would block the infrared signature of the target).

There are two increasingly fine target visibility modes for the FLIR. Neither is suitable for target acquisition — the broad area field of view, twelve degrees by twelve degrees is equated to looking through the cardboard tube of a paper towel roll; the other, finer view of three degrees by three degrees is like looking through a soda straw — but once pointed to a target acquired by the radar they will stay automatically locked on. A tracking rate of 75 degrees per second permits even low-altitude high-speed tracking.

The black-and-white picture of the target's infrared emissions seen in the FLIR is even more precise than that of the APG-73 in fine resolution (which is a single-digit number of feet, although the number will vary depending on conditions). On the F/A-18, the image is projected up onto the HUD or can be called up on one of the two DDIs. The other DDI can show the APG-73 radar return and the HI continues to show the moving map display.

The FLIR has other advantages. It will show targets such as armored vehicles under camouflage netting which do not block its infrared emissions. FLIRs can even see the traces of where a system has been from its impact on geothermal radiation. A laser target designation will show up as white hot on a FLIR.

On hot, hazy days in a desert, hot objects and hot terrain are harder to distinguish but the gunboat is an excellent thermal target for the FLIR because it is against the background of the water, allowing it to stand out clearly. Its engines are likely to be hot spots even if they are turned off and the gunboat is trying to appear inconspicuous among fishing dhows. The AAS-38B FLIR pod's integral laser rangefinder can both determine range and put a laser designator on a target.

Target Designation

Nickel Flight now splits for the attack. This is possible because the E-2C sees no hostile air threat to Nickel flight. The E-2C Hawkeye, standing off in the distance, uses its large dome-mounted APS-145 to watch for enemy fighters. If there was such a threat, the F/A-18s would not want to risk losing mutual support and the task would probably have to be assigned to a four-ship flight.

Nickel 02's task is to designate the gunboat by placing a laser beam from its under-fuselage designator pod onto it. Nickel 02 descends to 15,000 feet. Pointing the pod at the fine-resolution FLIR spot's location makes sure it is actually locked onto the target. The laser designation will stay, stabilized, as Nickel 02 flies a racetrack pattern until Nickel 01 is inbound on its base leg. Then, Nickel 02 will close toward the target at a 30 degree offset from the heading of Nickel 01's attack.

Nickel 02's back-seater (a pilot could do the same if the aircraft was an F/A-18C) handles the target designation while the pilot watches for any threats: a missile launch from the gunboat or enemy fighters that have evaded other sensors. Nickel 02 calls Nickel 01 over the UHF to let him know when the laser designator is locked on.

Such "buddy-lasing" tactics, in which one aircraft with a designator could be used to paint the target for the attacks of many other aircraft, date back to the initial use of LGBs over North Vietnam in 1972. These tactics have also been used in the Gulf War, when laser-designator equipped RAF Buccaneer attack aircraft provided target designation for LGB-armed Tornadoes when they switched to medium-altitude attacks. While the AAS-38B Nite Hawk FLIR pod, introduced into use on F/A-18s since the Gulf War, gives a self-lase capability, buddy-lasing still has the advantage of allowing the bombing pilot to concentrate on his attack. This is possible in relatively permissive air defense environments where there can be precise coordination between the two attacking aircraft. It is also practiced as a back-up technique in case an aircraft's designator fails.

Above: Bombs away! This F/A-18D from the VMAT-101 'Sharpshooters' training unit at El Toro, California has just released two free-fall Mk83 bombs, but is still armed with two pods of unguided rocket projectiles.

BOMB DAMAGE ASSESSMENT

Nickel Flight will do BDA as it pulls away from the target. Nickel 01 already has a good idea the gunboat as been sunk. As he and Nickel 02 pulled off the target, the FLIRs stayed locked onto the target for much of the maneuver. In a high threat environment, this would be used to provide BDA. It appears from the FLIR picture on the DDI visually that the gunboat has taken a direct hit. Nickel 01 calls the E-2C on the UHF voice radio and gives a preliminary report, using the day's brevity code words for complete success and no air defense fire.

"Hummer 1, Nickel 01. Broomstick, no mustard."

Tomcats and TARPS

Following the strike is an F-14 with a Tactical Air Reconnaissance Pod System (TARPS) pod containing three cameras, the KS-87, forward-looking or vertical, the KA-99 horizon-to-horizon panoramic coverage and the AED-5 infrared camera. F-14s with TARPS pods are the carrier battle group's long-

Above: The F/A-18D of VMFA(AW)-224 on the right is accompanied by an F-14 from VFA-84 'Jolly Rogers', based at NAS Oceana. VFA-84 was the first Tomcat unit to be equipped with TARPS (Tactical Air Reconnaissance Pod System).

Nickel Flight's BDA Pass

The E-2C now asks Nickel Flight for a BDA pass. If the target had been heavily defended or if it appeared that the first attack had alerted the defenses, this would not be done. But with the success of the attack, the E-2C asks Nickel Flight to circle around and make a pass, from a different direction, over the gunboat's position. This will give the F/A-18s the chance to use their radar and FLIRs to assess the damage they have done.

Nickel Flight's BDA pass is a repeat of its attack pass. Using the APG-73 radar in short-range fine-resolution mode, they can indeed see the gunboat is now only wreckage, an oil slick, and a life raft. The FLIR shows the same. Video-recordings of FLIR images will be taken from Nickel flight's aircraft back on the carrier to officially determine the results of the strike.

range eyes. The TARPS system lacks the precise resolution and mission-specialist reconnaissance pilots associated with a previous generation of aircraft such as the RF-8 and RA-5. It still does not have the real-time video and datalink to send its images back to the carrier while still in flight. They will be supplemented in a few years by F/A-18s with the multi-spectral Advanced Tactical Air Reconnaissance System (ATARS) which will have a datalink.

While the F-14 lacks the F/A-18's state-of-the-art surface search radar, FLIR and INS system, the F/A-18 has an upgraded LANTIRN (Low Altitude Navigation and Targeting Infra-Red for Night) pod with an integral INS and GPS system that allows targets to be spotted at longer range, even in degraded thermal conditions. Here, the F-14 is provided with an excellent beacon (and some IR masking) in the

Above: The variable-sweep wings of the F-14, developed for extended loiter performance and slow approaches, give a high penetration speed for bomb damage assessment. The 'NJ' code indicates a Tomcat from VFA-124 'Gunfighters', based at NAS Miramar.

Approaching the site of the former Iranian gunboat and the Silkworm sites on shore, now a smoldering pile of twisted scrap steel, the F-14's LANTIRN pod's long-range low-light television allows it to visually identify the subject of the reconnaissance pass. The same pod's integral INS can be pre-set with a course taking it over the TARPS subjects. Many TARPS sorties are carried out at night, with the F-14 crew using night-vision goggles.

As with strike itself, the tactics of the TARPS-equipped F-14s will depend on the situation. It will make its pass after the strike is pulling off the target (waiting long enough for the smoke and dust caused by the weapons strikes to dissipate) if it can be covered by "Iron Hand" F/A-18s and EA-6Bs. Alternatively, if another sortie is called for, the F-14 may use high-speed low-altitude minimum exposure tactics. In either event, it will normally be accompanied by another F-14 as wingman, looking for air and surface threats while the TARPS ship flies the course needed to get the photographs.

BDA proved to be a weakness of US airpower in the Gulf War. Many targets were killed multiple times, while others went untouched. The number of specialist reconnaissance aircraft available with sensors that could provide the high-resolution imagery able to determine which targets are dead and which simply lying low was limited. The Navy used TARPS, as they had in 1980s battles with Syria, Libya and Iran but once again it proved easier to have multi-mission aircraft than multi-mission aircrew. This is one reason why provision of a cockpit video recorder for F/A-18s has become a priority upgrade.

As Nickel Flight pulls off the target after its BDA pass, a new threat appears.

"MULTIPLE BOGEYS!"

Above: More store combinations for the F/A-18Ds of VMFA(AW)-224. In this case the nearer aircraft is carrying bombs, while the further aircraft has the AGM-45 Shrike anti-radiation missile for defence-suppression.

In the back of "Hummer 01", the E-2C controlling the strike, the Combat Information Center Officer (CICO) and two air control officers are monitoring the complete air picture. The on-board computers take radar inputs and IFF data and give each target's course, speed, and altitude. The computer will automatically assign each radar contact a track number. This information is automatically transmitted back to the carrier by Link 11 datalink. The three officers in the E-2C can access this information themselves by putting their light pens against each radar "blip" in turn. Course, heading, speed, and altitude will then be displayed on the screen.

The information can be transmitted to F/A-18s on a Link 4A datalink (in the future, a state-of-the-art Link 16 will allow a broad range of situational awareness messages to be linked to the HI in the F/A-18's cockpit). In this case, the vectors of the air control officer would appear as alphanumeric or symbolic instructions on a screen on a Link 4A screen that can be called up on the left DDI. However, the E-2Cs circuits and computers can handle a limited number of intercepts at any one time using this method, so they are providing Nickel Flight with radar information over the secure (encrypted by the KY-58) UHF voice radio link.

"Nickel, Hummer 01 has multiple bogeys, including one plus Benny at bullseye's 90 at 40. Vector 60."

This means the APS-145 radar has picked up what appears to be a flight of Iranian fighters that has entered the E-2Cs coverage envelope, probably climbing from a forward airstrip (MiG-29s are designed for rough field operations). "Bullseye" is the gunboat's position which the E-2C controller knows would be entered in the F/A-18's INS. He knows that the F/A-18's mission computer can quickly work out the offset and point its radar — which the pilot now switches to air-air model with a flick of the finger switch on the HOTAS — in the right direction. They are forty nautical miles from the target along the 90 degree azimuth. The E-2C wants Nickel Flight to fly at a course of 60 degrees to position themselves for a long-range AMRAAM shot.

"Benny" is the day's brevity code for an F-14 (given to the pilot before take-off on a color-coded card to be slipped into a transparent pocket on the flightsuit leg). This means that the E-2C's ESM has detected the air-air radar of an F-14 along the same bearing line as its radar has detected a flight of aircraft.

The E-2C controller suspects that this is an Iranian F-14, not one of the strike aircraft out

of position, but he needs to check to avoid a possible "blue on blue" shot-down. That is why the contact are still designated as "bogeys" rather than "bandits", which they would be if confirmed hostile. The E-2C will interrogate the bogeys' IFF. It will also call the F-14s providing the HVUCAP (high value unit CAP) protecting the E-2C, ES-3A and EA-6Bs, to make sure he is not vectoring Nickel Flight against them. Seconds count and a mistake that avoids losses to friendly fire can be just as fatal as the friendly fire itself. The only F/A-18 shot down in the Gulf War was lost in this way, hit with a missile fired either from a MiG-25 Foxbat-A or an SA-6 SAM launcher while an E-3 AWACS checked out a fast-closing bogey.

Nickel Flight Goes Air-To-Air

Nickel 01 calls Nickel 02, ascertains that he had also heard the E-2C, and makes sure he is positioned to keep up mutual support in any air combat. Nickel Flight is in combat spread, with both F/A-18s abeam about a mile apart, allowing mutual visual checking of each other's vulnerable six o'clock .

    In this loose formation, intended to permit visual search while allowing both aircraft's radar to search the location of the bogeys, Nickel Flight turns to the appropriate heading in response to the E-2C's vector. Nickel Flight is pointing their radar in the direction that the E-2C has determined the bogeys are to be found. In an instant, the HOTAS' radar and weapons switches are flicked from air-surface to air-air mode.

Datalinking

Data from the E-2C also comes over the Link 4A datalink displayed on the left DDI and repeated on the HUD. This shows the airspeed, altitude, and rate of altitude change called for by the E-2C in numbers. The command heading is shown on the DDI by a double chevron next to the appropriate number on the compass rose of the datalink display. The scale of the compass rose selected by the E-2C — 10, 20, 40, 80, 160 or 320 nautical miles — shows the distance of the vector.

    Meanwhile, the E-2C is vectoring the HVUCAP of two F-14s to back-up Nickel Flight. The F-14s, with the more sophisticated Link 11 datalink, can get complete data for an intercept from the E-2C's computer without having to go through voice transmission. Currently, F-14s are being re-

equipped with the even more powerful Link 16 datalink, which will be connected to the Joint Tactical Information Distribution System (JTIDS). Fighters with these datalinks will have the potential of receiving all the situational awareness information in their area of operations (using computer filters not to overload the pilot) from aircraft such as the E-2C or USAF E-3 AWACS.

    Meanwhile, Whale 01, the ES-3 ELINT aircraft backing up the E-2C, is following the action both over the voice UHF circuits and over its Link 11 datalink, same as on the F-14s. The ES-3 brings its UHF intercept capability to bear on any voice UHF transmissions that may be coming from the bogeys. The ES-3's ESM systems carry out a computer-directed scan on the Iranian Air Force's known UHF operational frequencies until they find vectors being passed in Persian. The system then pipes the intercepted data to a Persian-language linguist officer riding in the back of the ES-3. She recognizes it from the call signs as an F-14A directing two two-ship flights of MiG-29s. The ES-3 sends this information to the E-2C over the Link 11 datalink and UHF voice radio.

Above: One of many useful features of the F/A-18 is that air-to-air missiles can be carried in the form of AIM-9s on the wingtips and AIM-7s on the intake ducts, while leaving five pylons free for tanks and air-to-surface weapons.

QUICK DRAW OVER THE STRAITS

The F/A-18s are now searching for the bogeys with their APG-73 radars and "listening" for their air intercept radars with the ALR-67 RHAW gear, while closing rapidly with them in a head-on. This is a highly dangerous situation. The enemy is likely to be looking for them as well. While Iran's F-14As probably can no longer use their long-range AIM-54A Phoenix air-to-air missile — the shelf life of those sold them in the 1970s having expired — any Russian-built MiG-29s being directed by the F-14 will have long-range radar-guided AA-10 Alamo missiles.

Left: This F/A-18D from VMAF(AW)-224 is carrying a bomb and Maverick under one wing and a bomb and Shrike ARM under the other. The 'BM' tail-code again indicates liaison with VMFA-451.

Passive sensors usually have a longer range than active ones (whose electrons have to make a round trip). Nickel Flight gets an indication on their ALR-67 RHAW gear. It shows the signal of an air intercept radar of the same frequency as that of an F-14's radar coming from the direction of the E-2C's vector. Nickel 01 centers his radar search on that bearing, calling Nickel 02 to tell him of the contact and to keep a wide radar search, looking out for MiG-29s which may be trying a radar-silent approach, guided by the backseater in the F-14. The E-2C now sees the enemy changing course. He had been trying to manuever Nickel Flight into the beam of the enemy. Now, by turning toward their attackers, the enemy has set up a dangerous head-to-head tactical situation.

The advantage obviously lies with the first side that can detect and fire at the rapidly closing enemy. In air-air mode, the F/A-18's APG-73 radar has a maximum range of over 100 miles (less against fighters or cruise missiles). In air-to-air mode, the F/A-18 radar has velocity search (VS), range while scan (RWS), track while scan (TWS) and raid assessment mode (RAM) modes.

"Contact." A blip appears on the radar display on the right DDI in the F/A-18's cockpit, repeated on the HUD, which then resolves into a pair of aircraft. The APG-73 in air-air mode has better resolution than the more powerful but lower frequency UHF APS-145 on the E-2C. Detected at a range

gunnery solutions are also displayed as the computer quickly generates them.

Nickel 01 now calls Nickel 02 and the E-2C to make sure they are indeed seeing what he is seeing. This is the last chance for de-confliction, under the rules of engagement that have been pre-briefed for this mission. The E-2C now sends back, by voice and datalink, its response.

"Nickel flight, cleared hot."

The F/A-18, his aircraft's nose pointing at the threat, calls Nickel 02 to announce his attention of setting up AMRAAM shots. He assigns a different target to Nickel 02 to prevent both aircraft concentrating on a single

about of 45 nautical miles, the radar display indicates the altitude, speed, and heading of the target on the radar display called up on the DDI and HUD.

Once he has the enemy detected, Nickel 01 uses raid assessment mode (RAM) for target selection, as the radar can display up to ten bogeys and a choice of weapons. The radar mode is selected by a flick of a finger switch on the HOTAS throttles. The pilot also can manually adjust the elevation of radar search (especially useful when low-flying threats are being searched for).

The radar automatically locks onto two targets. Information on the target — speed, altitude, range, heading — appears on HUD and the DDI displaying radar returns. Dynamic missile launch zone and snapshot

enemy and letting the others home free. While doing this, the APG-73 radar display tracks all the targets. It can continue to track up to ten targets while engaging up to two.

In seconds, with the two sides closing head-on at a combined closure rate over 1,000 knots, Nickel 01's radar locks on to the target. The fire control computer resolves a targeting solution and provides a target indicator box on the HUD. This shows the pilot where the target is in space, even though it is far out of visual range: Slightly below and to his one o'clock. An "in-range" indication also appears on the HUD. When parameters permit the maximum probability of kill for the weapons selected — in this case, AMRAAM — the message SHOOT will flash on the HUD.

Above: The F/A-18 series is biased toward the surface-attack role. However, it is able to compete with dedicated fighters by virtue of its outstanding radar and cockpit, and its freedom from departures and engine surges.

"NICKEL 01, FOX ONE"

Above: Early weapon trials were performed by the Navy's VX-4 'Evaluators' at NAS Point Mugu, California. This has now been combined with VX-5 'Vampires' from NAWC, China Lake to form VX-9, also at NAWC.

The F/A-18 pilot pulls the pistol trigger on the stick and calls over the radio: "Nickel 01, fox one", to be answered by an the same call from Nickel 02. On both F/A-18s, an AIM-120 AMRAAM air-to-air missile leaps off the under-fuselage rail. The time to impact display appears on the HUD and automatically counts down. The AMRAAM is a fire and forget missile and will require no further guidance from the F/A-18.

The AMRAAM accelerates to Mach four. Its inertial guidance system keeps it on course, based on where the F/A-18's radar told it the enemy was heading at the instant of launch. Before it gets too close to this predicted position, the AMRAAM's own active radar seeker head turns on. This radar's acquisition basket, though small, is still large enough to acquire the target even if it is not where the F/A-18's computer has predicted it would be. Making a 30-g turn, the AMRAAM acquires a MiG-29, homing in on its radar return until its proximity fuze — highly sensitive to deal with the high rate of closing — detonates. The fragments and blast shoot out from the AMRAAM's warhead and, in an instant, the MiG-29 goes down. An instant later, Nickel 02's target follows it.

The fire control computer has automatically computed a shot at any other potential target. If Nickel 01 has more than one AMRAAM, he would now have the option of firing another

AMRAAM at the second aircraft. As it is, Nickel Flight turns away and repositions for a second attack, using Sidewinders if required. Nickel 01 now turns away from the heading toward the enemy fighters and Nickel 02, having fired its AMRAAM, does the same, keeping mutual support. The key is to get them into position to attack with heat-seeking Sidewinders and not to run into the enemy by staying on the same course (this was a drawback of the AIM-7M which is still in US service and not a fire-and-forget missile). One thing they definitely do not want to do is expose the vulnerable six o'clock of the F/A-18s.

Nickel flight, having broken away from the AMRAAM firing pass, dash to their two o'clock position, trading off airspeed for altitude. If the enemy has fired missiles at them, they will be pointed at empty sky when they arrive. If any surviving fighters keep closing, Nickel Flight should be able to roll in behind them.

The F/A-18 now points its nose back at the azimuth where the MiG-29 had been. On the HUD and the radar returns displayed on the DDI, the F/A-18C/D's computer had continued to update the position of the threat even when it was out of the APG-73s radar coverage. Putting its radar back into RAM, Nickel 01 does not see the MiGs. There are no more emissions on ALR-67 either.

The E-2C did not see the instant of the kill — the impact happened while its radar antenna was making a mechanical sweep — but was able to track the destroyed aircraft on their way to the Strait and even the ejector seats of the pilots.

"Nickel flight, Splash two."

Nickel Flight can now go out of burner — they are already short on fuel — and turn toward their original course. Nickel 01 calls the E-2C to ask about any other threats — the F-14 is still out there — and resumes a 360-degree visual search. Just in time to see a speck — a MiG-29 in full afterburner — climbing from the deck below and behind him, with another heading for his wingman.

Despite all the tools of situational awareness, the F/A-18 has just ended up with an armed and dangerous MiG-29 (and extremely angry, just having had his wingman shot down) at his five o'clock low.

The MiG-29s are the survivors of the two two-ship elements which each lost an airplane to Nickel Flight's AMRAAMs. They had dived for the deck after the AMRAAMs hit, dropping chaff. The E-2C's track continued on to the falling MiGs and the chaff cloud. Pulling out of their dives over the beach, the E-2C had not yet re-acquired them with its APS-145 radar. They were out of the radar coverage of Nickel Flight as they repositioned.

The MiG-29s had their radars off, and were directed by the F-14, which, not knowing Nickel Flight is out of BVR (Beyond Visual Range) missiles, is standing off, out of AMRAAM range. The MiGs were vectored under Nickel Flight and then told to pull up into a climbing attack, guided by the MiG-29's powerful internal IRST (infrared search

and tracking) sensor, intended to be able to detect even targets using electronic countermeasures. This sensor, like that on F-14D, is designed for air-air tactics. The F/A-18's pod-mounted AAS-38B FLIR is primarily air-ground. Nickel Flight is, for the first time today, at a tactical disadvantage.

Above and Below: The Sukhoi Su-27 ('Flanker') series is Russia's equivalent of the American F-15, but with more advanced air-to-air missiles.

THE HORNET'S ENEMIES

Modern fighter missions are not simply the white-scarf duel of fighter pilot vs. fighter pilot. This mission demonstrates that today's F/A-18 fights as part of an integrated mission that involves many different types of aircraft, missiles, and ships. This is required because its opponents range from fighter planes, to radar-guided and surface-to-air missiles, anti-aircraft artillery (AAA), shore-based Silkworm anti-ship cruise missiles and Chinese-built gunboats. This mission is a conflict of systems against systems.

One way for the mission to court disaster would be for it to underestimate its Iranian opponents. Many tend to remember the victories of the Gulf War as the expected result of US military intervention. The US military setbacks and ultimate defeat at the hands of North Vietnam, or even embarrassments such as the Syrian response to a similar carrier air strike in 1983 — two strike aircraft shot down for little appreciable result — have faded into history. This is a mistake. Third world threats with modern weapons, even if not state of the art, can still inflict painful reverses.

Below: The MiG-29 ('Fulcrum') is broadly equivalent to the F-16. The Russian aircraft is better armed and has outstanding low-speed handling, but is deficient in fuel volume and has a high cockpit workload.

The Iranian Military

In the 1980s, Iran and the United States have fought on a number of occasions. The failed US hostage rescue mission was followed by a number of clashes during the Iran-Iraq War, culminating in the accidental shoot-down of an Iranian airliner that overflew a US cruiser in action with Iranian small craft. The Iranian military is obviously not able to stand up to US on a one for one basis, but it is not without its capabilities, having survived the eight years of war with Iraq in the 1980s. Since then, oil revenue has allowed some rebuilding, with new Soviet and Chinese hardware coming in to join the survivors of the Shah of Iran's buildup of the 1970s. But this has not returned the armed forces to anywhere near the level of capability they had at the time of the Iranian Revolution. However, the range of equipment acquired will complicate the US planning process. The strike can expect to encounter aircraft, missiles, and radars from East and West alike.

Radars and SAMs

Iran has early warning radars and SAMs from the US, Britain, Russia, and China. Pre-Revolutionary US HAWK SAMs (Israel provided spares during the Iran-Iraq War) remain in service. These have been supplemented by Soviet and Chinese-built systems, the older Soviet SA-2 and its Chinese version, the HQ-2, long-range SA-5, self-

propelled SA-6 and the Chinese FM-80, based on the French Crotale. There have been reports of Russia making high-performance SA-10 SAMs available to Iran on the world market. Of these, the SA-6, though a 1960s design, remains a threat, due to its maneuverability and home-on jamming function. The HAWKs, despite their age, are also potentially effective. Perhaps the most significant SAM threat are the SA-5s, because they have the potential to threaten stand-off sensor platforms on which US medium altitude strikes depend. To prevent SA-5s putting aircraft such as E-2Cs and ES-3As at risk, they will be targeted for priority treatment by SEAD (suppression of enemy air defense) efforts.

The Aircraft

The Iranian fighters that the F/A-18 may encounter are US designs supplied to the Shah's government in the 1970s or Russian and Chinese designs that have been supplied since the end of the Iran-Iraq War. These last have been supplemented by Iraqi aircraft that flew out to Iran during the Gulf War in 1991.

Iran's first-line air-air fighter and attack aircraft are both Soviet designs, the MiG-29 Fulcrum and the Su-24 Fencer. While reinforced by ex-Iraqi aircraft in 1991, they remain limited in numbers: about 24-30 each. They are supplemented by about 25 Chinese F-7 fighters. The Iranian Air Force has a maximum of 200 US-built F-4, F-5 and F-14 fighters, but less than half of them are probably operational.

The Iranian government's dissatisfaction with its fighter force has been demonstrated by the fact that they were one of the few air forces in the world, in the 1990s, to have a non-pilot as chief of staff (he was killed in a plane crash in 1995). Iran has also created a second, competing, fighter force in the hands of the Iranian Revolutionary Guard Corps Air Force. Originally organized during the Iran-Iraq War with Tucano trainers (and thought to be trained for kamikaze missions), the IRGCAF now operates Chinese-built F-7 versions of the MiG-21 Fishbed and F-6 version of the MiG-19 Farmer.

Totalitarian regimes have traditionally had a hard time staying on good relations with jazz musicians and fighter pilots, two professions that require a great deal of both skill and independent thought for success and are not amenable to tight top-down control. Iran has been no exception. Many of the best Iranian aircrew who were trained in the 1960s and 1970s fled before the revolution. Many of those who remained have been kept out of the cockpit as politically untrustworthy. The latest generation of pilots reflects the limited ability to train pilots up to world standards. Many of those flying the newer aircraft, however, are believed to have been trained in the country of origin of their aircraft. This would give the Iranians access to equipment such as radar jammers or anti-radiation missiles and the tactics for their use.

FULCRUM AT FIVE O'CLOCK: CLOSE-RANGE DOGFIGHT

Above: Shown here with maximum external tankage and flight refuelling probe extended, this F/A-18D is assigned to VMFA(AW)-225 'Vikings' at NAS Miramar, the location for the 'Top Gun' movie and sometimes known as 'Fightertown, USA'.

Despite the F/A-18's high-tech equipment, what saves Nickel 01 is not any of the sensors, nor the E-2C, nor the ES-3, nor the two F-14Ds coming up to reinforce, but the fighter pilot's swivel neck.

"Nickel 02, break hard right. MiGs, five o' clock low, five miles."

The F/A-18 jettisons its centerline tank and turns into the attack as hard as it can — its maximum G rate — because it has slowed down, it is close to its corner velocity of about 360 knots, the speed at which the combination of rate and radius of turn makes it best for the F/A-18 to maneuver. A hard break means that the two F/A-18s are going to turn as tightly as they can, "yanking and

banking", even though they have to trade off altitude and airspeed, despite the acceleration of the F/A-18's engines — now thrown back into afterburner to get Nickel Flight out of their disadvantaged position. At 360 knots true airspeed, the F/A-18 is incredibly maneuverable. Pulling an 8G turn at an 82.8 degree angle of bank, it has a radius of turn of 1,500 feet and a rate of turn of 20 degrees a second.

The Iranian MiG-29 pilot, operating with his radar off to avoid alerting the F/A-18's RHAW gear, despite the F-14's vectors and his aircraft's excellent internal IRST, was just as surprised to see the F/A-18 as Nickel 01 was to see him. His switches were not set up and he was not in position to take advantage of his Russian-made helmet-mounted missile sight and AA-11 Archer heat-seeking missiles. This gives him a capability to engage targets throughout his forward quarter, up to 45 degrees off boresight. Had both MiGs been able to set up a shot at Nickel flight, they would have likely been successful hunters.

Now taken by surprise by the F/A-18's sharp break toward them, the MiG-29 starts to overshoot. To reduce the rate of overshoot, the MiG pilot cuts the throttles and pulls back on the stick. He continues to climb, jettisoning his large 440-gallon centerline fuel tank, with which he is limited in the amount of "g" force he can pull as he maneuvers. But even without the 4-g limitation of the drop tank, the MiG-29 is now at a disadvantage. The Russian fighter was not designed for sustained high-g maneuvering like an F/A-18.

Right: An early MiG-29 with four Vympel R-60 (AA-8 Aphid) short-range missiles and two of the company's R-27 (AA-10 Alamo) medium-range missiles. The R-60 has been discarded as ineffective, but R-70 remains in front-line use. It has an effective range of 70 nm (130 km).

This underside view of an F/A-18D from VMFA(AW)-533 shows Lockheed Martin Lantirn pods on the intake stations and four free-fall Mk83 bombs on the wing pylons, while retaining external fuel and provision for AIM-9 Sidewinders.

THROWING THE FIGHT INTO THE VERTICAL

Left: Trading speed for height, this F/A-18C comes from VMFA-251 'Thunderbolts', another Beaufort unit.

Nickel 01 has saved himself from immediate destruction at the hands of the MiG-29 by the classic tactic of turning into the attack and forcing the attacker to overshoot. Now Nickel 01's pilot has to make an instantaneous decision, whether to go after the MiG-29 closest to him or to go "two on one" along with Nickel 02, engaged with the other MiG-29 after Nickel 02 has broken hard into the MiG's attack.

If Nickel 01 does not press home an attack against the MiG that attacked him, it will probably pull up in its climb, reverse direction in an Immelmann turn and be back with its AA-11 missiles pointing at Nickel Flight, a danger once again.

Nickel 01 goes after the MiG that overshot its attack on him. The F/A-18's fast engine spool-up speed gives it the capability to respond quickly to the attack. While the MiG, in its zoom climb, may have had the initial energy advantage, it expends this while trying not to overshoot Nickel 01.

The F/A-18 pilot uses a fingertip to shift the weapon select button on the stick. Another fingertip move on the throttle sets up his radar for automatic target acquisition. Pulling his air-air pistol trigger on the HOTAS stick will now launch the AIM-9M Sidewinders on his wingtip.

The F/A-18 and MiG-29 are now in a vertical rolling scissors. Each aircraft is now reversing direction, either by turning or by a barrel roll, trying to get the enemy to overshoot and make themselves vulnerable. This gives an advantage to the fighter with the best acceleration in a climb at first and, then, to sustained rate of climb.

The F/A-18 is an excellent close-in dogfighter due to its thrust-to-weight ratio and slow-speed flight characteristics. Even at high angles of attack, the F/A-18 pilot can rely on his engines to keep responding precisely as he wishes. The F/A-18's all-variable leading edge also gives it an advantage. It allows the wing aircraft to continue to fly at high angles of attack without stalling. This and the flaps are part of the computer-controlled "live wing". The pilot never has to worry about the F/A-18's trim in air combat. The wing is constantly trimming itself. Meanwhile, the radar, once set in air-air mode by a flick of the HOTAS switch, is trying to acquire a lock-on on the MiG. Nickel 01 is a single-seater, but its pilot has a full crew of systems working for him on board.

THE DECIDING FACTOR

Despite the importance of these control and weapon systems, the F/A-18's real advantage is in the skill of the pilots. Nickel 01's pilot has had the advantage of the world's finest training and experience. In addition to his pre-deployment training against US Navy aircraft, this particular pilot has practiced air combat maneuvers (ACM) with Luftwaffe MiG-29s off Sardinia, as have many F/A-18 pilots before heading off to cruises that may take them into harm's way.

The MiG-29 pilot, however good his natural skills, serves in an air force where resources and flying hours are both in short supply. He cannot be expected to reach the same degree of air combat maneuvering proficiency that is common in US F/A-18 units.

In the cockpit, as he is turning "canopy to canopy" with the MiG-29, the F/A-18 pilot feels the physical effects of high-g maneuvers, grunting to relieve the pressure against his abdomen. Each additional "g" in effect

doubles his body weight against his muscles (one reason why fighter pilots "pump iron" whenever possible). However, the HOTAS controls means he only has to move his wrist and the finger. The HUD means he does not have to look down in the cockpit, only at the MiG.

The pilot does not, however, keep focused on the MiG. He would be able to do this if fighting with Nickel 02 in close support, but since the fight has ended up as two "1v1" dogfights, he must "check six" to make sure another MiG has not joined the fight. The MiG gains a temporary advantage when it turns when the F/A-18 pilot is looking behind, as his maneuver will lag a fraction of a second until his head swivels back. Following the MiG, however, the F/A-18 pilot's training allows him to anticipate when the MiG is going to reverse, positioning himself inside the turn.

Above: Not something to tangle with at close quarters, a MiG-29 with a helmet-mounted sight and Vympel R-73 (AA-11 Archer) missiles is a formidable opponent.

VECTOR ROLL ATTACK

Above: Designed to combine Mach 1.8 capability with excellent controllability at a carrier-compatible touchdown speed, the F/A-18 sacrifices transonic acceleration.

The F/A-18 is able, because of its superb low-speed maneuverability, to stay inside the MiG-29's turns. The MiG-29's poor rear-angle cockpit visibility makes it hard for the pilot to keep his eyes on Nickel 01, but the F/A-18 pilot, cockpit toward his adversary, is able to keep the MiG in sight.

As cuts inside the MiG's turn, to prevent overshooting, the F/A-18 pilot's finger hits the speedbrake control on the HOTAS throttle. The F/A-18's big speedbrakes — another requirement of carrier operations — deploy from the upper fuselage in front of the rudders in a fraction of a second, slowing the airplane without having to wait for the engine to spool down. An overshoot prevented, the speedbrakes are instantly retracted by another flick of the switch.

As he comes toward the MiG, the F/A-18 pilot makes a vector roll — also known as a barrel roll — to cut inside the turn. To stay inside the MiG-29's turn, Nickel 01 pulls up

above the MiG-29's turn and rolls inverted and inside him. The MiG-29 quickly reverses the direction of his turn, rolling through 180 degrees and turning as hard as the MiG can without stalling, trying to throw off the F/A-18's aiming solution. The tide of battle has turned. The MiG-29 is now looking to disengage (he's also short of fuel, having jettisoned his external tank), by diving back down for the deck in a split-S, half-rolling and pulling into a vertical dive. He never gets the chance.

The F/A-18's vector roll has put it in position to fire an AIM-9M all-aspect heat-seeking air-air missile. The pilot makes one final maneuver to get the acquisition box on his HUD — now set for AIM-9M heat-seeking missiles — onto the MiG. For an earlier generation of heat-seeking missiles, the MiG would be too close, forcing the F/A-18 to try for a hard-to-achieve gun kill, but the AIM-9M has a reduced minimum range. The

uncaged seeker heads of the Sidewinders, on the rails, acquire the MiG-29's engines. The SHOOT indication flashes on the HUD. The pilot hears a low growl in his earphones. He pulls the pistol trigger and gives a radio call that he has just fired a heat-seeking missile.

"Nickel 01, fox two."

After a fraction of a second delay for the system to process the commands, an AIM-9M Sidewinder comes off the F/A-18's wingtip rail. Its seeker head was already focused on the MiG-29, locked onto the correct source of IR radiation. In a burst of rocket acceleration, the Sidewinder overtakes the MiG-29, its laser proximity fuze detonating the warhead close to the MiG-29's tailpipes.

Fortunately for the MiG-29 pilot, one area where his aircraft is unquestionably superior to the F/A-18 is in its ejection seat. The Russian-built K-36 seat separates him from the crippled aircraft and leaves him dangling from his parachute, considering the fact that

the Straits of Hormuz are to sharks and sea snakes as Central Park is to cyclists and skaters on a sunny afternoon.

The F/A-18 pilot calls the E-2C, "Nickel 01, splash one Fulcrum," and asks for a vector to Nickel 02.

Above: The virtually unswept wing of the F/A-18 facilitates stores carriage and release. In this case external fuel and wingtip Sidewinders are combined with FLIR pod, a laser-guided GBU-12 Paveway II, and an AGM-65E Maverick.

Left: The violent maneuvers demanded by air-to-air combat often leave fighters at low altitude, at reduced speed. Here they are vulnerable to SAMs from shoulder-fired heat-seekers to advanced optically-guided weapons like the BAe Rapier system.

SAM SHOT

During the close-range dogfight with the MiG-29, Nickel 01 has not only lost visual contact with Nickel 02, but has put himself within the lethal envelope of an Iranian SA-6 SAM battery on the beach below.

Nickel 01, rolling away from the burning MiG, is not looking at the parachuting Iranian, but for his wingman and the other MiG. He experiences the well-known feeling of a pilot trying to re-establish overall situational awareness after focusing on a target directly in front of him, that of being all alone in a vast sky. He starts now to listen for the E-2C's calls, which he had focused out in the last few seconds of the fight with the MiG-29. Fortunately, the HUD will cue him as to any radar contacts that are in his forward arc by putting a box around the spot

Right: Diving steeply, this F/A-18D is carrying four Mk83 bombs, a centerline tank, and a FLIR pod on the right-hand intake station. The 'ED' tail-code indicates membership of VMFA(AW)-533 'Hawks'.

where the contact physically is, even if it is out of visual range.

What he hears is to aural warning tone from his ALR-67 RHAW gear, followed by a warning call from the E-2C, telling him that both its own ESM and that on the ES-3 have detected a fire control radar. Because the aural warning tone associated with a lock-on came on within a few seconds of the radar first being detected, it is likely that the SAM battery started tracking the F/A-18 with an electro-optic sensor (a long-range TV camera) as soon as it broke away from the fight with the MiG, and has now cued the fire control radar, which was able to quickly acquire a track. It also shows, once again, how quickly the hunter becomes the hunted. The 1995 shoot-down of Captain Scott O'Grady's F-16 over Bosnia by a similar missile, though in cloud and poor visibility conditions, shows that even threats with less than state-of-the-art electronic sophistication can still master sufficient ECCM (electronic counter-countermeasures) techniques to kill today's fighters.

Looking around, Nickel 01 sees not his wingman, but the flash of a SAM launch from a camouflaged self-propelled launcher. Even with the electronic warning provided by the ALR-67 RHAW gear on board the F/A-18 (which, unlike earlier-generation RHAW, can

detect the SA-6's Straight Flush radar's continuous wave signals), and warnings being passed from the E-2C and the ES-3, the most important step to surviving a missile shot is often seeing the flash of the launch on the ground. This is why flying above an overcast over enemy territory remains as potentially deadly today as it was a generation ago over North Vietnam. In the Gulf War, an F-14 was "scarfed up" by an old-design SAM, an SA-2, emerging from an overcast. Here, as during the MiG-29 attack, the pilot is well served by the F/A-18's excellent all-around visibility, far better than that on the aircraft it replaced. High up in the bubble canopy, far forward on the fuselage, the pilot can see in all directions, above and below.

Once again, the F/A-18 is at a disadvantage. To survive this threat will require him to use maneuver, chaff, and ECM together, all within the few seconds it will take the SA-6 to reach him. First, the maneuver: the F/A-18 breaks hard into the missile, rolling inverted. The F/A-18 dives, trying to get under the SAM's flight path. The pilot keeps his eyes on the missile. But he needs to pick his course of action early and stick with it. Otherwise, the F/A-18 will end up doing a "funky chicken dance", first one way, then another, and be within the SAM's terminal homing envelope.

DROPPING CHAFF

As the F/A-18 dives, the pilot uses a fingertip to push the "chaff/flare" selection button on the throttle to "chaff", then hits the dispense button. This starts to automatically dispense chaff from the ALE-47 chaff/flare dispenser.

The ALE-47 at pre-set intervals ejects chaff cartridges out of the rear of the F/A-18. Chaff is made up of thin metalized mylar film cut into hair-like strips in lengths equal to the wavelength of hostile radars. The ALE-47's chaff cartridges have each been filled, and the launcher itself has been pre-loaded to reflect the most likely threats the F/A-18 may encounter. A several-second program of chaff cartridges launched from an ALE-47 will cover a number of SAM guidance wavelengths.

This means that rapid blooming chaff clouds are blossoming behind the F/A-18 as it starts its maneuver, trying to interpose the clouds between itself and the maneuvering SAM. The missile may then home in on the larger return of the chaff cloud.

Left: A US Marine F/A-18C from VMFA-312 heads down range. The Hornet is very maneuverable even when carrying ordnance.

JAMMING

The F/A-18 would be in a much better situation if it had a modern jammer, with computerized power management, linked automatically to the RHAW gear. Such systems are switched on when entering the area of operations and operate largely autonomously. However, its on-board jammer is an older type, the ALQ-126B. Only a few F/A-18s have the more modern ALQ-165 Advanced Self-Protection Jammer (ASPJ) which has long been sought after by the F/A-18 community (and which have proven effective in service over Bosnia) but has been blocked from broader deployment by Congressional critics after a troubled development.

The ALQ-126B is not a state-of-the-art ECM system. It differs from the USAF's jamming pods in being an internal design, requiring much less cooling and power. It is a deception jammer. Every time its transponder is triggered by a pulse from an enemy fire control radar (of the type on the ground or in the nose of an active-homing missile), it

transmits back an enhanced pulse, but injects a small but increasing time delay. As a result, what the fire control radar is seeing is, as well as the "skin paint" of Nickel 01, a much larger and juicer target, moving away from the F/A-18's position, which is in fact the signal being broadcast by the ALQ-126B. Because this target is moving in the direction of the chaff cloud, the combined effect is to seduce the missile seeker away from the aircraft, breaking its lock-on, and onto the chaff cloud.

Nickel 01, diving behind the spurious returns from its jammer and chaff bundles now should appear not naked and alone in the sky, but a small and inconspicuous target hurtling out of the way.

The F/A-18 pilot, pulling hard G, has one more trick. He flicks the transmit switch, but

SHOULDER-FIRED SAMs

Nickel 01 has, in his dogfight with the MiG-29, lost mutual support with Nickel 02. In his dive to evade the SA-6, he has now ended up at low altitude and short on fuel. Before he can climb back to talk to the E-2C, report that he has bingo fuel — the pre-briefed fuel state requires him to break off the mission — and try and rejoin Nickel 02, the pilot finds that he is vulnerable to man-portable heat-seeking surface to air missiles.

The pilot of Nickel 01, climbing back to altitude, realizes that the crews of the fishing boats he can see in the Strait are unlikely to be friendly. He quickly switches the chaff/flare dispenser program on his throttle to the "flare" position and initiates a pre-programmed sequence of infrared decoy flares. Each of these flares, burning at several thousand degrees centigrade, is intended to jam the infrared seeker eyes of a heat-seeking missile.

The man-portable SAM is one of the most deadly threat faced by modern combat aircraft. In the Gulf War, Soviet-made SA-16s destroyed more coalition aircraft than any other single type of air defense weapon. One of these is fired at him by a gunner on one of the fishing boats, just off the beach, that the strike has striven mightily to avoid.

To the pilot of Nickel 01, the corkscrewing smoke trail catches his peripheral vision, looking just like the simulated "smoky SAM" launches he would have been familiar with

from "Strike". While active warning systems are currently being deployed for the US military, today's fighter pilots must rely on visual sighting of heat-seeking missiles. Because of this, US tactical aircraft will try and fly either above or below the effective envelope of these SAMs and drop flares on a pre-set program when they cannot.

As with the SA-6, the F/A-18 maneuvers to evade the missile. He dives for the surface to the Gulf, turning hard — but not too hard for there is no altitude to give up — into the missile, keeping his nose toward the target rather than his vulnerable tailpipes. The missile, fired upwards at the F/A-18, may now

Above: Flying over inhospitable territory, this F/A-18D is loaded with both bombs and rocket pods. Unguided rockets are still an economical weapon against large and relatively soft targets.

switches off the KY-58 encryption device. He transmits, in the clear, over the UHF,

"Nickel 01, Magnum".

This is the call for firing a HARM. He hopes that the Iranians are monitoring that particular frequency and will react by turning off their fire control radar. The large-scale use of HARMs has already made the Iranian SAM battery nervous. They are aware that even if they manage to hit this target, it will serve to highlight their position for a HARM-shooting Iron Hand F/A-18 or EA-6B.

That the SA-6 missed the F/A-18 was not surprising. Even when the SA-6 was a new weapons system, in the 1973 Arab-Israeli War, its overall probability of kill was down in the single digits. Today, to kill a modern fighter, even one with a less than stellar jammer, it requires the element of surprise. In the clear skies over the Strait of Hormuz, this was hard to achieve.

Above: Another Miramar-based unit is VMFA-323 'Death Rattlers', one of whose F/A-18Cs is shown here with eight Mk82 bombs and a centerline tank. Note the automatic leading edge flaps, significantly augmenting maneuverability.

not be able to "push over" and search below it to acquire its heat emissions, especially if it is against the surface background radiation (although some environmental conditions, such as sun glint on water or a hot desert, work much better at fooling heat-seeking sensors). The SA-16, its seeker eye jammed by the emissions from the flare, does not pick up the F/A-18.

Nickel 01 is sorely tempted to flick his weapons switch to guns and demonstrate the power of the F/A-18's integral M61A1 Vulcan 20mm cannon. With the accuracy provided by the HUD and the fire control computer's real-time correction represented by a CCIP, a single strafing pass would reduce the fishing boat from which the missile came to driftwood. However, such an attack is not briefed under the rules of engagement and, more to the point, Nickel 01 is now very low on fuel indeed.

Again, it is not surprising that the single SA-16 missed Nickel 01. To be effective, man-portable SAMs must be used en masse. Even the most effective SAMs of this type only yield a kill perhaps once in six launches. Had the SAM hit the F/A-18, it probably would not have proven fatal. All three of the F/A-18s hit by man-portable SAMs in the Gulf War made it back, and some were back in action within a day. The missile hits tended to knock out one engine. The F/A-18's high level of systems redundancy (especially hydraulics) and the titanium keel between the two engine compartments made it likely that only a lucky hit from such a missile will bring it down.

Left: Loaded for defense-suppression, this F/A-18D of VMFA(AW)-121 'Green Knights' is carrying a Shrike anti-radiation missile under the right wing. First fired operationally by Israel in 1967, the AGM-65 Shrike is still in use.

HEADING HOME

Above: Its mission successfully completed, the Hornet heads back to its nest, still supported by AEW aircraft and tankers.

The missiles evaded, Nickel 01 is vectored to a tanker by the E-2C, and refuels with little to spare. The E-2C and the forward Aegis cruiser may put Nickel 01 through delousing maneuvers, having him orbit a point for IFF interrogation or asking for specific maneuvers, making sure that he is not an Iranian trying to follow the strike home. He may even be asked to fly-by a pair of F-14s (probably the two upset at Nickel Flight for poaching 'their' Fulcrum kills).

The F/A-18 navigates back to the carrier. The inertial navigation system will bring it back most of the way. Despite the violent maneuvers the F/A-18 has been undergoing, its INS is known for being highly accurate. With GPS updates, it should get Nickel 01 close to the moving target that is his home. The TACAN VHF radio beacon and the DME (Distance Measuring Equipment) show the bearing and range to the carrier. If this does not suffice, once the carrier's radar picks up Nickel 01, he can ask for steering instructions.

APPROACHING THE BOAT

The F/A-18, its navigation task solved, has to land. Having switched frequencies away from Hummer 1, Nickle 01 calls in the carrier's strike control, and reports his distance outbound of what all carrier pilots call "the boat" and fuel state, giving it in the form of plus or minus a brevity code figure changed for each mission.

Strike control now gives Nickel Flight a recovery radial and directs the pilot to switch to the marshal frequency to receive instructions on where and how to hold in a marshaling stack to wait his turn for landing.

If Nickel 01 has sufficient fuel remaining, he will be directed to a stack of aircraft each in a marshaling racetrack course, each 1,000 feet in altitude apart. Nickel 01 holds at 20,000 feet and 35 miles astern of the carrier. Aircraft with battle damage and low fuel states will obviously have priority. A tanker will be flying a pattern near the carrier to refuel those kept holding too long or who need fuel for an extra approach.

Flying overhead on its way to the marshaling stack, Nickel 01 now sees "mother": the carrier. There is one more difficult maneuver to be performed, landing on the carrier deck. Any carrier landing is hardly routine flying. It is little wonder that

US Navy pilots measure their operational experience in "traps", the number of arrested carrier landings they have made. Nickel 01 now tests his landing instruments to make sure they are functioning.

Above: Returning strike aircraft do not always approach from the anticipated direction and their communications may be damaged. With many US aircraft in the air, good communication is essential to avoid a 'friendly fire' tragedy.

Left: As Nickel Flight completes its mission, two more F/A-18s depart on a long range attack. Armed with a GBU-12B 500-lb laser guided bomb under each wing, they carry 315 gallon centerline tanks and a 330 gallon tank under each wing.

FINAL APPROACH ON AUTOMATIC

Above: F/A-18Cs from VFA-195 'Dambusters', based at NAF (Naval Air Facility) Atsugi in Japan.

Below: Hornets first saw combat in 1986, when VFA-131 and -132, and VMFA-314 and -312 struck at Libya from the USS Coral Sea (CV-43), shown here. Like the USS Midway (CV-41), this carrier could not take the F-14, and thus had four Hornet squadrons. Coral Sea has now been replaced by the USS Abraham Lincoln (CVN-72).

The carrier will sequence landings so that each aircraft can leave its place in the marshaling stack at one-minute intervals and all can be recovered with the minimum delay. In daylight, the recovery can be done in strict EMCON: radio silence. When Nickel 01's turn comes for landing, he will acknowledge to the carrier and start to descend.

The carrier's approach control, functioning much like that at any non-floating airbase, has a number of options when directing the F/A-18 pilot to make his final approach.

The F/A-18 has an ARA-63A instrument landing system (ILS) for all weather approach guidance. It receives azimuth and elevation guidance data from a directional transmitter on the carrier. The ILS data will be shown on the HUD and HI. The ILS can be used as part of the Automatic Carrier Landing System (ACLS) or it can be used to provide steering cues on the HUD with the two "needles" that show elevation and azimuth deviation. If the two needles form a precise cross, the pilot is on the glide slope and on the center line.

The F/A-18 is also equipped with this ACLS. An uplinked computer on the carrier provides steering commands through the Link 4A datalink. The commands may be coupled directly into the F/A-18's flight computer for fully automatic approaches to touchdown. Alternatively, the pilot may use the information displayed on the datalink (displayed on the left DDI of his instrument panel), to fly a manually controlled approach. As with radar and other data, that from the ACLS is repeated on the HUD to allow the pilot to keep his eyes out of the cockpit and looking at the carrier on his final approach.

ACLS approaches are long and straight-in. When the carrier's approach control is forced to have aircraft turn or manuever between the marshaling stack and final approach, it cannot always maintain good "on-speed" performance, and so may decide to have the pilot fly the approach manually.

In an ACLS-controlled Mode 1 approach, Nickel 01 would descend from its place in the marshaling stack toward the carrier at a rate of descent of 4,000 feet per minute, after calling the carrier to tell them he is leaving marshaling. Once the pilot has established the desired airspeed and descent rate, the F/A-18 will follow the commands of the ACLS

system as shown on the Link 4A display. He will also set the warning functions on the radio altimeter to prevent his going below authorized altitudes.

As the F/A-18 passes through 5,000 feet, he is "on platform". The ACLS system will hold the pilot at that altitude until it sets up a new rate of descent. The pilot calls "platform" and shallows the descent rate to 2,000 feet per minute. While on platform, the F/A-18 continues to close with the "back end" of the boat, getting into position to pick up the glide slope.

The ACLS' azimuth steering commands will be displayed on its HUD and HI. This will show the traditional ILS "needle" on the F/A-18's HUD. If the pilot were told to fly the ACLS approach manually, he would rely on these "needles" for constantly updated glide slope and azimuth. He would fly the F/A-18 so that the aircraft symbol on the HUD was lined up with a cross-hairs formed of the two needles.

At eight to ten miles astern of the carrier, the F/A-18 is configured for landing. The flaps, landing gear and tailhook are lowered. If this is to be an ACLS approach, Automatic Throttle Controls (ATC) are engaged.

The pilot reports his position to the carrier while exactly 1,200 feet above the Gulf of Oman.

"Nickel 01, ten miles."

The F/A-18 is now on course to an entry window to landing. It must pass through this 630 foot by 10,000 foot "window" at four to eight mile range to pick up the highly directional signals from the carrier.

Six nautical miles from the carrier, the pilot goes through the pre-landing check list. The traffic control (T/C) mode to the ACLS is now coupled and the radar altimeter engaged. The datalink is now capable of taking control.

The pilot can, however, either select ILS "needle" steering or full manual control at any time. The pilot checks whether the aircraft is receiving commands — the aircraft should be straight and level — and gives the radio call to the carrier, to report that the F/A-18 is coupled to the ACLS system.

"Nickel 01, coupled. "

Above: Homeward-bound Hornets, in this case F/A-18Ds of VMFA(AW)-224. The mission may be over, but a carrier landing is always a potentially hazardous operation.

CALLING THE BALL

However, the carrier now decides, to keep spacing for the many fuel-low aircraft of the strike, it will have Nickel 01 leave the ACLS approach and carry out a Mode II approach, when the pilot will manually keep the ILS needles centered while the controller on the carrier provides this information over the radio as well. The HUD will display the proper angle of attack (AOA), which is critical to the Navy style of final approach. Once the correct AOA is set up, the aircraft does not flare before touchdown as in a normal landing, but touches down at that attitude (hence the need for a reinforced landing gear). He will control final approach with power.

"Paddles", the carrier's landing signals officer (LSO) (the nickname comes from the days of piston-engine fighters when they waved paddles to direct aircraft aboard) will be directing the F/A-18 over the voice radio. Visually assessing the F/A-18's approach from his vantage point near the arresting wires next to the carrier's flight deck, the LSO will call the incoming Hornet.

"Nickel 01, on the glide slope, lined up, call the ball."

Nickel 01 replies, giving his aircraft type and fuel state.

"Nickel 01, Hornet, ball, two point oh."

If the pilot did not see the ball, the call would be "Clara" instead. The fuel state lets the carrier know that he could probably do another pass without having to refuel from a tanker if he is waved off and has to go around for another approach or if he "bolters", which happens when his tailhook fails to engage the carrier's arresting gear and his attempted full-stop landing becomes a touch and go as the

pilot goes flying off the angled deck to go around again. It also lets the arrester crew know the aircraft weight to set the arrester gear to receive.

"Roger, ball, 27 knots," the LSO acknowledges, giving wind over deck.

This is "calling the ball" which means that the F/A-18's pilot has transitioned from instruments — such as flying the needles — to a purely visually guided approach. This is a difficult transition, especially at night. It takes about 20 seconds from calling the ball to touching down, and it is that 20 seconds that sets the carrier pilot apart from all others who fly high-performance jet pilots. Only the carrier pilot has to end it by landing at a base which is moving, rolling, and pitching.

"Ball" is short for meatball, the yellow disc light indicator of the Fresnel lens system that provides visual guidance for carrier landings. If the reference "meatball" light was higher than the horizontal row of green lights, then the pilot knows he is too high.

With the aircraft trimmed for approach, he takes power off (making sure not to take off too much). If the "meatball" light is below the green reference light row, it means that the approach is too low and he must add power. If the meatball appeared red, then the plane is dangerously low and must add power or risk a ramp strike, when an undershooting aircraft flies into the ship just below the flight deck in the most spectacularly fatal recurring mishap in naval aviation.

Keeping the meatball lined up with the horizontal indicators is "flying the ball", changing power either manually or through the F/A-18's automatic throttle and adjusting course. Flying the ball is done either manually or through the ACLS. "Spotting the deck" is the opposite of "flying the ball" and occurs when a pilot is looking at the carrier's deck and trying to land by visual reference rather than looking at the meatball. Spotting the deck can lead to a low approach. It can become a ramp strike.

Above: Happy landing - an F/A-18C of VFA-86 'Sidewinders' touches down with puffs of burnt rubber on the deck of the USS America, passing an F-14 parked on the starboard side of the deck.

TOUCHDOWN

Watching the approach are the LSOs: not just a single officer, but a team of pilots. They can flip on red waveoff lights — the switches for which they hold high over their heads when the deck is not set for landing and by their sides when it is — to send around again any airplane whose approach appears unsafe. They are in voice radio communication, through telephone-like handsets, with the pilot after he calls the ball.

Guiding the F/A-18 to the carrier deck is done visually. If the F/A-18's wingtip lights form a straight line with the small approach light on its nosewheel landing gear door, the LSOs can tell it is at the proper approach attitude. Experienced LSOs also use the noise of the engines to monitor the approach.

The whole procedure is being watched and monitored on the Pilot Landing Aide Television (PLAT), which is used for later critique and evaluation. The Navy's carrier squadrons grade every landing and keep a daily-updated "league table" posted in each squadron ready room to show standings. Consistent underperformers may be brought before a review board to see whether, despite the large investment in training them, they should not be found another line of work before they break an even more expensive airplane.

The F/A-18 pilot is now monitoring glide slope, line-up and airspeed. F/A-18's excellent acceleration helps with any power additions required to maintain them. With the F/A-18, the response is near instantaneous. This allows a pilot to redeem an otherwise bad approach with more power.

When the F/A-18's main wheels touch down on the flight deck, the pilot will immediately push the throttles forward to go to full military power. This way, if the F/A-18's tailhook fails to engage any of the carrier's four arresting wires — each connected with an arresting gear engine assembly with the tension adjusted to each different type aircraft and weight level — the F/A-18 will take off again on the angled deck, with the pilot announcing "bolter, bolter, bolter" on the approach frequency of the radio. He will then fly a traffic pattern around the carrier and try again.

This time, the F/A-18's tailhook catches the number three wire. In two seconds it decelerates to a standstill. The arrester cable and its attached engine limits it to less than 200 feet of deck roll.

The F/A-18 pilot now quickly pulls the throttles back to idle, raises flaps, disengages the wire. Nickel 01 is now sitting in the middle of the landing area of the angled deck, "fouling the deck" for the next plane in the approach pattern until he gets out of the way.

Guided by a yellow-jersey plane director, Nickel 01 makes an immediate right turn out of the landing area onto the flight deck. Passed from one yellow shirt to another, Nickel 01 is directed to taxi to a parking spot at the edge of the flight deck. Responding to arm signals from a yellow shirt, the pilot folds the F/A-18's wings. As it pulls into a parking space, blue-shirts deftly emerge from the flanks of the F/A-18 to chain it down onto the parking spot.

There is now one more checklist to do, that for shut-down. All the electrical systems are

Below: The Hornet's landing gear clearly displayed by this F/A-18C of VMFA-134.

powered down in proper order. Finally, the pilot turns off engines and makes safe the ejector seat. The F/A-18's brown-shirt plane captain will be waiting with the crew ladder to help the pilot down. He may have already heard word passed from "strike" about Nickel 01 two MiG kills and a gunboat sunk. The F/A-18 will keep its MiG kill markings for the rest of its career.

But after initial congratulations, the main task of the plane captain is to collect aircraft data allowing maintenance to correct any faults and make the F/A-18 operational again as soon as possible. The F/A-18C has an automatic data storage capability for recording maintenance and flight incidents data, and by reviewing this the plane captain will know if there are any repairs called for.

Later, there will be celebration, including a traditional wetting down (with water, US warships being officially dry) of the MiG killers. But now, as the pilot regains his sealegs on the rolling deck, he goes to his squadron ready room for debriefing. BDA reports will be reviewed to see if there is a need for an immediate follow-up strike.

After the last aircraft of the strike lands, two F-14s are launched to reinforce the CAPs in case of Iranian counterattack. An S-3B and an SH-60F launch to search for surface or subsurface threats. A KA-6D, despite having

flown multiple missions already that day, waits, fully manned, in case it is needed to launch to refuel any of the aircraft still airborne. Nickel 01's mission may be over, but that of the carrier continues.

Above: Its task completed, this Hornet is parked with wings folded to wait for tomorrow's mission, while an F-14 smokes its way down to the carrier deck.

Left: The air group's mission continues. The reliability of the Hornet's systems enables a high sortie generation rate to be maintained.

Picture acknowledgements

The publishers would like to thank the following organizations and individuals for supplying photographs for this book.

6: Aviation Photos International (two). 7: Randy Jolly/McDonnell Aircraft. 8: Bob Munro/Randy Jolly/Randy Jolly. 9: Randy Jolly/Aviation Photos International/David Isby. 10: Randy Jolly. 11: Randy Jolly (two).14: Aviation Photos International. 13: McDonnell Aircraft. 16: Aviation Photos International. 17: Aviation Photos International. 18,19,20: Randy Jolly. 21: US DoD/Aviation Photos International. 22: Aviation Photos International/Jane's Information Group. 23: Randy Jolly/US Navy. 24: Jane's Information Group/US Navy. 25: Jane's Information Group/Aviation Photos International. 26: Bob Munro. 27: Jane's Information Group. 27: Bob Munro. 28: Randy Jolly/US DoD/Tony Holmes. 29: Bob Munro/Jane's Information Group (two). 30: Aviation Photos International. 32: Randy Jolly. 34: Canadian armed forces. 35: Randy Jolly/Nellis AFB PAO. 36: Randy Jolly. 37: McDonnell Aircraft/Randy Jolly. 38-43 : Randy Jolly. 44: Nellis AFB PAO/Aviation Photos International. 46: Randy Jolly. 47: Randy Jolly/Aviation Photos International. 48: Randy Jolly. 49: Aviation Photos International (two). 50,51: Randy Jolly. 54: Aviation Photos International. 55- 63: Randy Jolly. 68: Randy Jolly. 69: Bob Munro. 70: Randy Jolly. 71-73: Randy Jolly. 74: US DoD. 75: Bob Munro (two). 76: Bob Munro. 77: Bob Munro. 78: Randy Jolly/US Department of Defense. 79-80: Randy Jolly. 81: Bob Munro. 82: Aviation Photos International. 83: Randy Jolly/British Aerospace. 84: Randy Jolly. 85-86: Randy Jolly. 87: Aviation Photos International/Randy Jolly. 88: Aviation Photos International. 89: Randy Jolly/McDonnell Aircraft. 90: Randy Jolly/US DoD. 91: Randy Jolly. 92-94: Randy Jolly. 95: Aviation Photos International/Randy Jolly.